CHANGE YOUR LIFE IN 3 MINUTES

THE REVOLUTIONARY METHOD OF A MULTIMILLIONAIRESS

CHANGE
YOUR LIFE

in 3 Minutes

REGAN HILLYER

CHANGE YOUR LIFE IN 3 MINUTES

The Revolutionary Method of a Multimillionairess

ISBN   978-1-5445-0437-7 *Paperback*

978-1-5445-0438-4 *Ebook*

This book is dedicated to all of the people on this planet who wish to change their lives rapidly...

CONTENTS

....

INTRODUCTION

....

I know. I completely get it. You already think I'm insane.

Change your life in three minutes?

It's impossible.

It's ridiculous.

It's crazy.

It works.

Just three minutes—really? Who can change their life in three minutes?

You can.

I did.

I changed my life in just a few minutes each day. I am living proof it works.

You can change your life in just three minutes a day.

I'm going to show you how to do it.

I'll teach you the tools you need to go from setting goals, to actions, to achieving your success.

First, congratulations are in order. You've already taken the first action toward changing your life. You bought this book. It will show you the process to take control of your life, just a few minutes at a time.

As you delve into this book, you'll learn it's often the small actions that generate the biggest results. The small action of buying this book will generate big results for you, if you invest your three minutes each day.

We live in a world where time is everything. Time is the most precious and most sought-after commodity. Everyone is busy. Whether you're a single mum juggling two jobs, an executive CEO, or a student with a side hustle; you're busier than ever.

Life is literally flashing us by.

Second by second our precious time ticks by.

Everyone wants more time. It's the one thing everyone craves more of. Unfortunately, once it's gone, you can never get it back.

Don't waste the precious commodity of time.

Wherever you're at right now, **I know you have dreams.** I know you have desires, and I know you're ready to change your life.

I also know that your time is precious.

This book is designed so you can *change your life piece by piece*, by reading for just three minutes a day.

As you invest time in yourself, you'll reap rewards and benefits as you work toward your dreams and life's desires.

Think of this book like a life playbook. In each section, you'll learn about one piece of your life puzzle, and define how it fits into your ideal life. Using the playbook, you'll know what you want and how to get it.

You don't have to read the entire book from start to end. Although you certainly can, if you'd like.

This book's design allows you to dip in and out of it daily.

You can flip through to wherever you'd like to put your focus, or simply open the book at random and allow yourself to be intuitively guided.

> *We are conditioned to believe change is hard, that it's difficult, that we have to struggle through and work really hard to create change.*

Expand your mind for a moment and consider this:

Change is instant.

Change is intentional.

Change can happen at a rapid speed.

If you choose it.

And I know you already have. So, let's get started. Remember how I said the book is designed to allow you to dip in and out of it, as you want? Well, that's true...mostly.

The first section of the book breaks down, step by step, how to create rapid change in any area of your life.

Read the "Critical Steps" section first!

The Critical Steps cover the building blocks you'll need for all the other sections in the book. After you've read the Critical Steps, you can feel free to dip around as you desire.

This book will show you how taking daily action allows change to happen quickly. Consider an Olympic gold medalist. A gold medal, without a doubt, will change an athlete's life. For many sports, it takes less than three minutes to win (or lose) a gold medal.

Yet it's the **daily action** leading up to the win that is the most important (and necessary) element for success.

To help you with this daily action, there are questions and tasks at the end of each section that will guide you into developing exactly the kind of life you want to live.

You need to take the time to do this work.

It's essential you do this so the true power at the heart of this book can begin to take root firmly in your life.

Without the work, how can you expect to get long-lasting results?

So, if you can commit right now to taking action when prompted, feel free to go on and dive right in.

So, are you ready to completely change your life?

Just give me three minutes of your day.

Three. That's it. Deal?

Let's go...

CRITICAL STEPS!

....

Okay, I need your attention for slightly longer than three minutes. Just this once, I promise! There are some important things we need to cover before you can dive deep into the rest of the book.

There are five simple (but critical) things you need to know.

These five snippets are keys to ensuring you get the life-changing results you want.

Please, don't just read these five key elements. Instead, absorb them, breathe them in, allow them to become part of you and your mindset. If you forget them or lose sight of them in the future, refer to them. Give them the attention they deserve, as they will impact the level of change you create.

Let's dive right in.

#1: YOU ARE RESPONSIBLE

Your mindset is everything.

Everything! If you are truly able to grasp the depth and importance of that statement, all our work here is done, and you can close the book. Just kidding—mostly!

Let me explain.

You are the creator of your own reality. You are in control. You are in the driver's seat. Everything you do or don't have in your life right now, you are responsible for.

Take a moment and let that sink in. You have complete control of your life. You are responsible for what you have (and don't have) and you can change that—in an instant—if you desire.

Let's talk a little more about reality. Your reality is what you perceive exists.

The reality of your life in this present moment is a result of all your past decisions, thoughts, beliefs, and actions.

Your reality is full of your experiences and what you've seen. Your reality is viewed through your perception, which is comprised of your thoughts, beliefs, and actions.

Like it? Great.

Don't like it? Too bad.

There's nothing you can do to change it! As with every new second that goes by, that reality becomes the past. And last time I checked, the past doesn't exist.

I know! That sounds weird, doesn't it? What? You could swear the past was a real thing?

Well, go on—if your past is that real, then prove it. Hand it to me right now. Go on—hand me your past.

Oh, you can't?

Maybe you're starting to agree that your past doesn't even exist. And even if you don't agree the past doesn't exist, **you must agree you can't change the past.**

All you can do is start to change the present.

Now THAT, you are in control of.

In fact, each new second is a new second chance. A second chance to think different, to act different, to be different.

This is your chance to change your reality. To change your life.

If you're not entirely satisfied with your current reality, and you'd like to see some different results in your present situation, here's what you need to understand at a deep level.

Mindset is everything.

> *You are the only one responsible for your own mindset. Hence, you're the only one responsible for your own present reality!*

To create a different present, we need to cultivate a different mindset.

Why? The answer is simple.

Your thoughts become things.

Everything that shows up in your physical, external reality was first created internally.

Good, bad, ugly—ALL of it! If you could only realize right now how powerful you truly are. You create your reality.

You are in control. You are responsible.

▌ *Now here's the thing—it is easy to spiral out of control.*

It's easy to play the victim.

It's easy to deny that you're in control.

It's easy to pull out the "poor me" card.

However, relinquishing your responsibility won't get you what you want. It's not the magic secret to getting the different present you want. Denying you have control over your life won't give you the life you desire.

All we can do is start to change our present.

The present is what matters.

Every second, you have a choice to make—the choice to be entirely responsible for your life in that moment, or, to not be responsible.

You can live by the effect of what is happening TO you, instead of creating the life you desire.

People who are not responsible for their mindsets are not responsible for the results in their life. They **react** to what happens to them in life. They are victims to life and deny they have any control over what happens to them.

People who are entirely responsible for their mindsets **create their present reality** instead of reacting. They are entirely responsible for their results in life. They choose to accept responsibility for their life and their present. They consciously create the life they desire.

You can either be responsible for your mindset or be a slave to it.

You can control how you respond to situations in your life, or you can choose to react to situations after they occur.

The choice is yours.

> *Take a moment and consider how you're currently responsible for your mindset.*

Let's review a quick example of the difference between responding and reacting to a situation.

> *Jocelyn and James work in the same department of a large company. They've heard rumors their department will be targeted next month for layoffs, and they're concerned about their future and security with the company.*

James reacts to the rumors by working extra hard for his boss, resulting in longer hours at the office. He's tired, stressed, and feeling out of control. His wife is frustrated with his short temper when he finally returns home after twelve hours at the office, and his kids have noticed a change in their father. Everyone is on edge, waiting to find out if dad will keep his job.

Jocelyn responds to the rumors by considering her position in the company. Although she is relatively comfortable she's not going to be laid off, she thinks through her goals. After careful consideration of her best interests, she decides to pursue employment with a more stable firm. She begins by updating her resume and initiating contact with other firms. She starts networking with friends in the industry over lunch, to find out if anyone knows of any opportunities.

Do you see the difference in how Jocelyn and James handled the same situation at work?

In every moment, we get to choose how we will handle every situation. Will we react (usually out of emotion), or respond (usually after thinking the situation through)?

List one time you reacted to a situation and you wish you had handled it differently. Explain how you could have responded rather than reacted.

#2: YOUR BELIEFS SHAPE YOUR REALITY

Now that you're clear that mindset is everything and you are in control, let's dive deep into how to start to shape your new reality.

We mentioned in the last section that your thoughts become things.

Yes, your thoughts become reality. Ultimately, your thoughts stack up over time and create beliefs, which can either be extremely powerful or detrimental to your results.

Let's think about this for a moment. Your thoughts create tangible results in your life.

Here's why.

If we go a layer deeper into this, here's what you need to realize:

Your beliefs influence your actions, which influence your results.

So, if you want to change the results you're getting in life, then you need to change the action you're taking. And you won't be able to change the action you're taking until you learn how to rewire your beliefs.

Look at it this way. You set out to try something new. Skiing, for example.

If you've never skied before, perfect. And if you have skied, I want you to imagine you're about to try skiing for the first time.

Confident, you head up the mountain, put on your skis, jump on the chairlift and off you go. You're standing at the top of the mountain and you have no idea how to ski down. You take a deep breath, a leap of faith, and then physically leap.

Only to fall flat on your face, bruise your behind, and eat a mouthful of snow.

▨ *Skiing is NOT fun, is what you decide in that moment.*

But you need to get down the mountain. So, you pick yourself up and attempt to ski for a second time. This time you fall faster and harder.

▨ *I'm TERRIBLE at this, you decide.*

Of course, as your level of belief drops lower and lower, you try less and less to make it work. Ultimately, the result of skiing down the mountain gets worse and worse.

See how it cycles?

Now, let's imagine something different. Let's say you head up the mountain for the first time and decide to make a different decision.

Instead of trying to figure this skiing thing out by yourself, you decide you're going to get an instructor.

The instructor shows you the basics of how to get down the mountain, you follow their instructions, and you take it piece by piece. You feel in control and in that moment, you decide...

Hey, this skiing thing is great, I'm really good at it!

And with a newfound belief that you're good at skiing, you put more and more effort in. As your belief increases, the aligned action increases, and sure enough, your results get better and better with effort.

You've created a mindset cycle here too, except this one is in an upward spiral, not a downward one!

How many times in your life have you gotten stuck in a downward spiral because you've been taking the action, but haven't been able to change your beliefs?

I can hear what you're asking: so HOW do I change my beliefs?

The answer is simple.

Choose to think something different.

A belief is just a thought—a thought that you're generally pretty solid on. A thought that you tend to think over, and over, and over again. Beliefs affect every aspect of our lives—from the information we take in, to how we perceive events.

What if you could simply choose to think something different?

Because you have a choice, at every given moment.

Don't think you're good enough?

▋ *What if you chose to believe that you were?*

Don't think that money is easy to create?

▋ *What if you chose to believe that it was?*

Don't think that you deserve a loving relationship?

What if you chose to believe you deserve all the love in the world?

You get to choose.

Change your thoughts, change your beliefs, change the action that you take, and watch your results compound.

Tackle one thing you wish you could "think differently" about and describe what you would change. Consider how you would respond to the situation and the changes you could make in your beliefs to create your ideal life.

Now, list two things you can do to make that happen—today!

#3: DAILY CONSISTENT ACTION COMPOUNDS SUCCESS

Generally, people think to have success in any area of your life, you need to do something drastic, extreme, or risky.

Although that's one way to achieve big results, there is a much easier way. You can manifest success in any area of your life—without the pressure and risk.

So, how do you manifest success?

Through daily consistent action.

Success, in any area of your life, is a compound result of small actions taken daily. Those small actions build a foundation of consistency that increases rewards.

It's true whether you're looking to achieve results with your health, relationship, or career—the same principle is valid. Daily and consistent action breeds success, exponentially.

It's just like compound interest. Compound interest is impressive because of the much **higher yields** it offers. Just as a tiny bit of interest, compounded daily, adds up, so does consistent and daily action. In fact, daily consistent actions **add up to success.**

So, what are you doing daily to create the results you want? Take a moment to think about a goal you want to achieve. Yes, right now.

Let's say you want to release twenty pounds of weight. You don't want to lose it, because you never want to find it again. You want to release it with the intention of it being gone forever. (Remember, our words create our reality, so let's **be specific and accurate** in stating what we want.) Now, ask yourself, "What am I doing daily to move closer to this goal?" **Think about it.** Take notes if necessary—this is important.

Once you know exactly what you're doing each day to make your dream your reality, consider what else you could do. Ask yourself, "What more could I be doing daily to accelerate (or compound) my result?" Next comes the second part of daily consistent action.

You need to do it.

Make a commitment to yourself to complete those small actions each day to achieve your results.

As you read more of this book, you'll see a series of daily processes that will accelerate and compound your results. **You'll see results** if you consistently and genuinely give them the daily time and attention they require.

The best part? You start small.

Even if the daily action is small, **it still adds up** if you're consistent with daily action.

You don't have to set goals of working out for four hours a day to release that weight. A high-intensity workout for just ten minutes every day can accomplish tremendous results.

Let's examine that a little more closely. What if instead of setting your goal to ten minutes a day, you set your daily goal to working out for an hour a day? Instead of starting small, you decided to take massive, extreme action in the direction of your goals.

What may happen?

You go to the gym on the first day and start to run. Because you haven't exercised in a long time, it's difficult. Scratch that—it's torturous.

But, as you set your mind to that goal, you run, and run, and run. You keep running even when you just want to quit.

You reached your daily goal. You made it!

Yay, right?

But what do you think happens the next day?

Well, besides not being able to get out of bed, you're probably not going to work out today. You might decide to rest for a few days, and then try again.

> *Extreme and drastic action actually hurts your progress. Before you know it, the few days have turned into a week. Then you are back to square one and aren't moving forward at all.*

That was a basic example, but the same mindset shows itself in **every** area of life.

That's why I suggest working on your mindset for a few minutes each day.

How many?

Well, three minutes, of course!

Sure, you can build that up over time, as your mental muscles get stronger.

In the meantime, **three minutes each day, consistently,** for thirty days is exponentially more powerful than even ninety minutes once a month.

Daily consistent action breeds success.

To get the most out of this book from this moment forward, commit to it. Commit to taking consistent daily action.

Just three minutes at a time.

> *List one small thing you can do every day this week to move closer to your goal. Provide details on the daily consistent action you will take to move closer to your goal.*

Now, do it. Every day, for a week. Remember, you need to commit to repeating the consistent daily action, every day, to compound success.

#4: OUR LIMITS = OUR ONLY LIMITS

There will be times in life, and while reading this book, that you want to give up. You will have days where you don't want to do the work you know needs to be done. You will have days where acting is inconvenient. There may be days when it all feels too hard.

Guess what?

Success is not convenient.

Success isn't easy.

Success requires daily action.

We all have the same twenty-four hours in a day. However, it comes down to us to decide how to use our precious hours. And remember, I'm only asking for a tiny bit of your day.

Just **three minutes,** actually. That's just two-tenths of one percent (0.2 percent) of your day. That's it. Just a teeny-tiny part of your day to achieve your ideal life.

Why do some people achieve massive success while others don't?

We all have the same 1,440 minutes each day, so why the big difference in outcomes?

The answer is simple.

You're either trapped by your limits or you are creating results.

But guess what? You can't do both.

When I say limits, I mean the limits in your own mind. Fear, self-doubt, lack of confidence, a lack of action, negative self-talk, self-sabotage—sounding familiar?

Remember, you're in control, and your thoughts become your reality. That means you're not only responsible for the success you create, but also for the limits you create internally as well.

Let's be clear.

Everyone has limits. Yes, everyone.

Everyone feels fear, sometimes.

Everyone doubts themselves, sometimes.

Everyone thinks negatively, sometimes.

What separates the successful from the not-so-much?

Successful people recognize their limits and move past them. They **deal with** the issues, and then use them to fuel their success.

Instead of allowing limits to control them, successful people choose to control their limits. They recognize they have a choice in how they deal with those limits.

That's right. You have a choice.

You have a choice in how you deal with your limits, so you can reach your goals. The limits we place on ourselves are the only limits we have. So, if you create them, you have the power to dismiss them—rapidly.

Let's talk about an example of limiting ourselves. Shannon, a recruiter for a major healthcare company, dreamed of opening her own recruiting company, specializing in flexible work schedules for physicians and nurses. She spent time each night working on her plan. Instead of watching television or going out with friends, she put her time and passion into her plan to create her dream company. One day she decided to show her plan to her mentor, the owner of the recruiting company she worked for. Shannon was very excited to share her vision and couldn't wait for her mentor to affirm all the hard work she'd completed on her dream.

After reviewing her business plan and details, her mentor was not supportive of her business plan. Her mentor pointed out all the potential pitfalls—many of which Shannon had already considered, but a few new ones popped up during the conversation. The mentor explained he didn't think the concept of "flexible" scheduling for healthcare workers was possible. It went against most traditional thoughts on scheduling, especially in healthcare facilities. He just didn't see how it could work, he said.

Shannon felt she had no choice but to scrap her plan. She didn't see how she could move forward with the plan without her mentor's support. In talking it over with a good friend, Shannon realized she didn't want to walk away from the plan. She seriously considered every potential pitfall and problem her mentor had brought up. She realized they were issues that all new businesses could face, but that didn't mean she wasn't going to try. Shannon decided her mentor didn't need to see how it could work, because Shannon could see it.

Shannon refused to limit her plan to only those solutions other companies had used before. She was committed to finding a better solution when scheduling healthcare professionals. Having worked closely with healthcare professionals for years, she knew what they wanted and what they didn't. She knew having scheduling flexibility was very important to her best healthcare workers. She knew she could provide that.

Shannon went on to build one of the premier healthcare recruiting and staffing companies in her state. Her firm is now one of the largest employers in the area, simply because employees **want** to work with a firm that considers their scheduling needs. Her biggest fear turned into her firm's biggest recruiting asset.

This book will guide you through exactly how to deal with and overcome your limits, to ensure you're working toward your ideal life.

> *Take a moment and think about the limits you have placed on yourself. List two limits you've placed on yourself recently.*
>
> *Then, consider how you can release them. Explain one way you can dismiss each of those limits in your life.*

#5: KNOW WHAT YOU WANT

I know one of the core reasons many people don't **achieve their desires** is because they don't **know what they want.**

I don't mean generalities.

> *"I want to be financially independent."*

I mean specific—nitty-gritty, down-and-dirty specifics. In order to get what you want, you need to clearly and specifically, in great detail, clarify exactly what you want.

> *I want to have X amount of money in the bank and have two of my highest yield credit cards paid off within six months.*

But, it's not just about one area of your life, is it? You want **success in all aspects of your life.**

You're a whole person. You're not just a bunch of compartments labeled: health, wealth, and family. You're a complex individual with your own personality, dreams, and desires. Each compartment interacts and affects all the other parts of your life.

Keeping that in mind, you don't just need to be clear on the details of what you want. You also need to think about how that will affect all aspects of your life.

It's important to maintain other areas of your life while achieving your goals. Unfortunately, it's common to "drop a ball" when juggling a lot of them at the same time.

The good news? You can have it all—on your terms. You can have exactly the life you desire. But, you have to stand up and actually claim it.

And, you guessed it—you can't receive what you want unless you clearly know what you want.

So, get clear. Get crystal clear on the exact life you desire to be living.

Write it out in whatever way works for you. Maybe you journal or write in bullet points—it doesn't matter as long as you unleash it. Get it all out and detail exactly what you want from life.

Focus on your big vision.

Ask yourself, "If I was to live my dream life and have everything I desire through every aspect of my life, what would that look like?"

Write your answer in the raw, real, and unfiltered way that is truly you.

Write from the standpoint in the present that you already have it all. You're living your dream life. What does it look like? What does it feel like?

"I am so happy and grateful to be in a committed, amazing, and loving relationship."

"I am so thankful to be financially independent and contributing to our savings each month."

"I am full of joy because I love my work. I look forward to work and love what I do."

"I am pleased with my athletic intentions, and I'm running my first marathon this month."

Your mind doesn't know the difference between dreams and reality, and the sooner your mind can see this big picture vision as a reality, the sooner it will manifest in your life!

Don't worry about "'how" right now. We'll get to how you can create that reality. Trust the process and simply focus on locking in the big vision.

Choose to overcome any limits that block you.

When you start thinking about something that will hold you back, think differently.

Think about ways around the problem, issue, or challenge. Find solutions rather than focusing on the problem. Think creatively about ways you could resolve it, rather than focusing on the negative aspect. Thinking about solutions shifts your focus to a problem-solving focus where we think outside the box to find solutions.

Recognize and release negative thoughts.

Don't dwell on thoughts such as, "I don't deserve that."

Release that limit and move on. Consider, instead, that you deserve exactly what you desire.

Bring yourself back to the big vision, exactly as you'd like it to be. The sky's the limit, so get thinking.

Think without limits.

The only limits are the limits you create. Feel unlimited. Why start with a smaller version when you can go straight to creating the big picture?

Be unlimited.

Some details you may want to consider when detailing your dream life include:

- Family
- Business and Career
- Wealth and Money
- Intimate Relationships
- Relationships with Friends
- Fun and Recreation
- Passion
- Health
- Mission and Purpose
- Contribution
- Emotions and Mindset
- Mental State

Well, what are you waiting for? It's time for you to go deep and declare your ideal life. Find your big picture vision of what you desire. Detail exactly what you want and describe your desired life.

So, ask yourself again.

> *"If I was to truly live my dream life and have everything I desired through every aspect of life, what would that look like?"*
>
> **Have fun!** *After all, it's your dream.*

Take a few moments and detail what your dream life would look like. Remember, be specific.

UNDERSTANDING HEALTH

....

> *"Take care of your body. It's the only place you have to live."*
>
> —JIM ROHN

Health is the first section of this book for a great reason. Without your health, what do you have?

Nothing.

Literally, nothing else matters if you don't have your health.

You can create all the wealth in the world, have the most amazing family, or have all the freedom you've ever desired, but none of it counts if you aren't able to enjoy it all!

Unfortunately, many people these days take their good health for granted and choose not to focus on it. Until they find themselves in pain or suffering, they assume all is well. But waiting until something goes wrong to focus on health changes our focus from responding to reacting. In other words, it's too late to respond, and you must react to the health crisis at hand.

I encourage you to choose to **think differently.**

Choose to make your health a priority.

Choose to make your health a priority now.

Instead of being reactive to health challenges as they appear, choose to take control of your health, now.

Consciously create your health. Just as we create our reality in other areas of our lives, we can adjust our health by our actions and beliefs.

> *If you had to put a number on your health right now, with one being extremely unhealthy, and ten being absolutely perfect, where would your health stand?*

Whatever number you're at right now—that is your reality. That is your current health status. It's what you've tolerated and accepted until now. It will remain your reality unless something changes.

If you don't choose to make a different decision—if you don't choose to consciously change it—that will be your ongoing standard of health.

Is that what you want? Do you want your reality to remain the same way it is now? If not, where do you want to be?

> *Take a moment and consider, "Out of the same one to ten scale, where do I want my health to be?"*

Remember, you are in control of your health. You are in control of your results. It may be a strange concept to grasp, especially if you've spent your life reacting to health challenges or reacting when you're in pain.

Instead, take a moment and work proactively toward better health. Consider how you can get to where you want to be.

> *What exactly would you change or do different?*

You are in control of your health. Health is a mindset.

Take a moment and think about how you will achieve your health goals. Consider small, daily, consistent actions you can take to improve your health situation.

> *List at least three small, consistent actions you could take to change your health status.*

Trust that if you do the work daily, it is possible to shift your health. If you do the work, you'll have the results you want.

Remember, daily consistent action breeds success.

THE LANGUAGE OF RELEASING

> *"Successful weight loss takes programming, not willpower."*
> —PHIL MCGRAW

Since you're reading the section about releasing weight, I'll assume you're interested in releasing some weight. Whether you want to shed a few pounds, or even way more than that, it will shape your health.

I'm all for being in shape and loving the shape you are in.

However, first things first. Let's change our language when we talk about weight loss.

What do you do when you lose something?

- If you lose your keys, you look for them.

- If you lose an important presentation, you scramble until you find it.
- If you lose your wallet, you may be devastated.

We attach value to things we lose.

Whether you intend to or not, you miss out when you "lose" something. The meaning is inherent when you lose something—you want to find it again.

When we talk about lowering our weight—we really don't value those extra pounds. We don't want to (consciously or unconsciously) think we are missing out by losing weight.

If you focus only on losing weight, your mind may attach value to that weight. Your mind may want you to find it again.

A common definition of the word "lose" is to be deprived of something. If you were to release 5 pounds, would you feel deprived? Yeah, me neither.

Remember, our words are things.

Instead, shift your language. Choose to view that weight as something you want to release or shed. Choose not to view those pounds as something you want to "lose."

Shedding or releasing a few extra pounds is completely different from losing them.

Of course, changing our language is only the first step. There are **a lot of things** that must happen to release the extra weight. There are steps to creating change.

> *If I was to be at my natural weight, what would that be?*

> *How would I feel?*

> *What would be different in my life?*

> *List three things you can commit to doing to take action in releasing the weight.*

EXPLICIT BODY GOALS

> *"Most people have no idea how good their body is designed to feel."*
>
> —KEVIN TRUDEAU

Start by being crystal clear on what you're aiming to achieve. If you aren't clear on your outcome, you can't achieve it.

Maybe it's that you want to release some weight, maybe

you want to tone up more, maybe you want to be the perfect size for that new dress.

The first step, then, is to be very clear about what you're working toward.

What is your ideal body outcome?

Let's think about that.

- Is there a specific amount of weight you're looking to shed?
- How will you know when you've achieved it?
- For example, will you step on the scales and see a different number?
- Will your clothes fit differently?
- Will you look different?

Shut your eyes and picture yourself once you've reached your goal.

- What do you look like?
- What does your body look like?
- How are specific parts of your body different?
- What does your face look like?
- Are you smiling?
- How does the outcome make you feel?

It's imperative you paint this ideal outcome in as much detail as possible.

If you can see it, you will achieve it. The more detail you can see it in, the easier it is to achieve.

If you can't see it yet, keep coming back to this, day after day, until you can visualize it.

Then, take a moment and refine your body goals. Define exactly what you want to accomplish. Describe how it will make you feel.

> *List at least three small, consistent actions you could take to reach your body goals. Remember, be specific and detailed.*

BODY MINDSET

> *"To me, beauty is about being comfortable in your own skin. It's about accepting who you are."*
> —ELLEN DEGENERES

Next, let's look at what you **believe about your body.**

Remember, your beliefs create your reality. Your beliefs are responsible for the results (or lack of results) you have around your health and your body.

- What do you currently believe about your body?
- What have you told yourself about your body in the past?
- Do you believe you have a great body? Or not?
- What have you told yourself about shifting weight?
- Is it hard? Is it easy?
- What do you believe to be true?
- Are there any beliefs you need to shift to accomplish your goals?
- Are there any beliefs you can choose to think differently about?

Releasing weight can be easy or it can be hard. Which one do you want?

Choose to think different.

Remember, your thoughts are things. They create your reality. Your beliefs are responsible for how you act.

If you believe releasing weight is difficult—it will be difficult.

What positive new beliefs are you going to choose to bring into your life right now?

Whatever you believe to be true, will manifest.

- What if releasing weight was easy?
- What if you deserved to have an incredible body?
- What if you chose to be healthy?
- What if you chose to look and feel amazing?

Choose to think different. Choose to change your direction when it comes to your body mindset. For a change, think positively about your body and encourage positive self-thoughts.

Repeat after me:

I release weight easily and effortlessly.

I achieve my ideal body with ease and grace.

I look and feel amazing, because it is my birthright!

I will perform daily and consistent action to achieve my goals.

> *Take a few moments and think about what you believe about your body. Detail some of your body beliefs below.*
>
> *Are there any beliefs you want to change? Describe the beliefs you want to replace or change.*

RETHINKING OUR BODY IMAGE

"To fall in love with yourself is the first secret to happiness."

—ROBERT MORLEY

Sometimes, it's not our body that needs help—it's our image of it. Everyone has a body image—what they think of themselves.

Body image is described as the subjective image of one's own body.

The key word is **subjective**. Subjective means biased or influenced by your personal feelings and opinions.

In other words, your body image is not necessarily an accurate view of your body. It's skewed with your own personal views, perspectives, and yes, hang-ups.

We all have feelings about how we look.

We also have feelings about how we think others think we look.

Body image can range from very positive to very negative. You may feel good about specific parts of your body, while hating others. Body image also includes how you feel about your body—whether you see yourself as strong, confident, or attractive.

Some people accept the way they look and feel good about it. They have a positive body image.

Their appearances may not match other people's ideas about what they should look like, but they are happy with themselves and their appearance.

Having a positive body image is part of accepting how you feel about how you look. Part of that is about how you look physically, but that's not all of it.

There is more to positive body image than just how you look.

It's about how you make others feel, how you feel about yourself, and how you interact with others. It may involve how easily you move around and get things accomplished. How confident and self-assured you are can also be part of a positive body image.

People with a positive body image understand that how they look does not determine their self-worth. Their value and worth does not come from, and is not tied to, their physical looks.

Having a positive body image also means you see yourself as you really are. While you may not be happy with every single part of your body, people with a positive body image understand, accept, and even appreciate their differences.

Many people, though, struggle with their own body image. It can be difficult to work through all the emotions and feelings we have about our bodies.

A negative body image can develop when someone feels they don't measure up to an external ideal.

Let's think about that. A negative body image means they don't feel like they meet an external measurement or societal ideal. Unfortunately, our society and the media can place those measurements so high that no one can live up to them all the time.

People with a negative body image are often unsatisfied with their body image. But they may not see themselves as they truly are.

Their image of themselves is skewed.

If you have a negative body image, you may feel self-conscious or awkward. You may feel shame about your body.

We all feel disappointed in our bodies at one time or another—that is completely normal.

But, if you consistently have negative thoughts about the way you look, or the way you think other people see you most of the time, you may need to change your thinking. You may need some distance to gain perspective on yourself.

Having a negative body image can have a harmful effect on one's health and well-being. A long-lasting negative body image can affect both your physical and mental well-being.

People with a long-lasting negative body image are more likely to:

· Have anxiety or depression
· Suffer from an eating disorder
· Have difficulty concentrating
· Take unnecessary risks with their sexual health
· Cease exercising and other healthy activity
· Cut themselves off from social interaction

So, what do you do when it's your perspective that needs tweaking?

Think differently.

First, approach your body image from a different perspective. Instead of thinking about all the things wrong with your body, consider all the things that are right with your body.

- Do you love your hair?
- Do you have beautiful eyes?
- Are your legs just amazing?
- Do you have radiant skin?
- Are your abs just amazing?
- Do you love your chest?

What parts of your body do you view with appreciation?

After identifying some of your body parts with appreciation, consider your whole body image rather than focusing on specific body parts.

When do you feel beautiful or handsome?

What can you do to extend those feelings?

Try making a list of things you love about yourself. Include anything and everything you enjoy about you.

Do you sing well?

Are you funny?

Do you enjoy helping people?

Make a list of your positive qualities that have nothing to do with your appearance.

No matter what your positive qualities are, start a list. Read through it daily until you start to see some positive aspects of you.

When you're dealing with a negative body image, try to surround yourself with people who support you. Supportive people make you feel good about yourself. They don't trash you. They don't talk down about you. They build you up, especially when you're having a tough time.

Ask yourself, "If I was to truly love my body image, how would I be thinking/feeling differently?"

MINDSET TO CONSISTENT ACTION

"It's not what we do once in a while that shapes our lives. It's what we do consistently."

—TONY ROBBINS

Now that you're aware of your mindset regarding body image, it's time to take that new mindset and bring it into the physical realm by taking action. If you don't do anything different, then you won't see different results.

If you want different results, you need to act differently, consistently.

Take some time and think about these questions.

- What do you choose to do differently?
- What are you going to put into your body that will be different?
- How are you going to move your body in ways that are different?
- How are you going to choose differently?
- How are you going to make changes in your life to accomplish these changes?
- What specific strategies do you need help and support with?

This is your base action plan—and it's very important. To create the results you desire, you need to be very clear about how you will make it happen. Don't get stuck on getting ready. What's important is right now. With your new mindset, beliefs, and action plan, ask yourself:

> *What will I commit to doing today as part of my new daily ritual to move closer to my ideal body?*

> *Write out a minimum of three things you will commit to doing right now to move closer to releasing the weight that you desire.*

Of course, we all know that releasing weight doesn't happen overnight.

However, internal change can happen rapidly.

The more you repeat these exercises, the faster you'll see results.

Continue to put your focus and attention on creating change, and you will be celebrating successes. Remember, daily consistent action breeds success.

TAPPING INTO MORE ENERGY

> *"Your life either takes your energy or gives you energy. Set up your life so that it gives you energy."*
>
> —FREDERICK LENZ

One way to improve your health is by tapping into more energy. When you have more energy, then your body is more capable of healing and being healthy. You will have more energy to put into your life, so you can spend more time working on the things you want to achieve. The benefits of tapping into more energy really are boundless, so let's look at a few ways you can increase your energy levels.

When we allow ourselves to rest, our bodies and minds can revitalize. Think about how exhausted you are at the end of a long day. You go to sleep exhausted, but you wake up the next day feeling refreshed and alert, right?

When we sleep, our bodies can replenish. Our brains process the information gathered throughout the day, causing us to experience dreams. By dreaming, our brains can "catch up" and make sense of all the things we need to understand.

When we let ourselves rest throughout the day, maybe we go and lie down for a power nap, or practice some meditation, our bodies experience a similar state to sleep, even though we remain awake. By resting as much as we can, our energy levels will be maximized, giving us more creative energy to put into our daily lives.

How cool is that? It's so nice to take time out and relax, and now we know this will help us to improve our lives and achieve the things we want to. So, you can feel good about doing nothing, sometimes. Just be sure you monitor your amount of time resting, so you don't allow yourself to spend your entire day resting.

Commit to at least one rest per day.

DEEP BREATHING

Another way to tap into more energy is by conscious, intentional deep breathing. Most people breathe unconsciously. When you never stop to take a deep and conscious breath, your body and mind are never given a break throughout the day.

You might spend a full day locked up inside your head with all the thoughts of the things you have to do. Every now and then, jump out of your head and into your body, and take several big deep breaths. And while you're taking those deep breaths, try to sit for at least five minutes and focus on your breathing.

Those of you who meditate will know this exercise, and you will already know it reenergizes your body and your mind. In the beginning, this process can seem challenging, but in time, you will gain skill and find it easier to let your mind settle on the breath. It's also a great way to better understand yourself and find peace, but that's for another chapter.

Commit to doing a deep breathing session for a minimum of three to five minutes per day.

HEALTHY EATING

If you are eating food that is full of energy, your body is

going to absorb that energy and put it to use. If you are eating heavy foods that your body will use a lot of energy to process, that's more energy you won't have to keep yourself going. Eating light foods your body can digest easily means the leftover energy will be yours to use. Your brain will also be better able to remain concentrated on your daily tasks.

Eat as much as you like, however, make sure you are eating healthy meals.

If you're eating highly nutritious and healthy meals, your body will utilize that goodness for its own vitality. You can completely maximize your health this way. As long as the food you eat is good, you really can eat as much as you like. If your meals are light, your body will have no problem digesting and absorbing them. This is one of the easiest ways to maximize your energy levels.

Commit to putting lighter foods in your body.

EXERCISE

It might seem contradictory, but sometimes exerting energy can make more energy! When we do physical exercise, our bodies and brains increase their ability to handle more activity, so it increases our capacity for living.

It is possible to overdo it though, so gentle exercise is recommended when you first begin. Start with a simple walk, then maybe some jogging. Get yourself a gym membership and a few sessions with a personal trainer, so they can teach you the basics of strength and conditioning. Once you know what you're doing, set a goal of working out three times a week.

Unless you are working toward extreme physical goals, you only have to do fifteen minutes of exercise three times a week to see massive improvements in your overall well-being. That's less time than it takes to read the newspaper. Give your brain a break for fifteen minutes and push yourself to do some physical exercise.

> *What are three things you can do to tap into more energy? Commit to including three, fifteen-minute exercise sessions into your week.*

PURPOSE

....

> *"When you're surrounded by people who share a passionate commitment around a common purpose, anything is possible."*
>
> —HOWARD SCHULTZ

When you **love** what you do, it shows.

When you **love** where you are in life, it shows.

When you **love** who you are, it shows.

Finding and recognizing your passions in life helps you tap into your higher purpose. But, how do you do it? How do you find what makes you truly happy? How do you find what drives you? How do you find your passion and purpose?

First, let's figure out what purpose is, and what it isn't.

▌ *Purpose is the reason for which something is created.*

Do you believe you have a purpose? Do you believe you have a reason for being created?

I do. **I believe each of us has purpose and value.** I believe every person has at least one strong and undeniable purpose. Most people have many purposes. I'm not talking about how the barista's purpose is to get your morning latte correct. I'm talking about the purpose of their life. It very well may be that the barista's passion is to make the perfect latte—to give to others that moment of complete bliss as you sip the first exquisite taste. Or, it may be just a second job while they pursue their purpose of sculpting.

The point is, purpose, passion, and jobs don't always connect.

But when they do, watch out! Amazing things happen when purpose, passion, and work cohabitate. Amazing things can happen for you when you align your life, work, and passion with your purpose. Remember, daily consistent action breeds success.

▌ *Take a few moments and think about your purpose in*

life. Then, detail your thoughts about your purpose.
What do you think your purpose is? If you don't know,
how do you plan to explore your possible purpose?

PASSION

"To succeed you have to believe in something with such a
passion that it becomes a reality."

—ANITA RODDICK

What is passion? What does it mean? How does it affect
our lives?

Passion is defined as a strong and barely controlla-
ble emotion or enthusiasm for something.

Strong and barely controllable—that's descriptive, right?
Have you ever felt "barely controllable" about something? Have you ever wanted something so much that
it's almost uncontrolled enthusiasm? Have you ever seen
a spark come into someone's eyes when they talk about
something? Have you ever seen them get so animated
and excited that they're practically bouncing out of the
seat with excitement?

Have you ever heard someone talking about some-
thing they love, and you could feel the love through
their words?

That's passion.

Passion is enthusiasm that makes you get up before dawn to bake that fresh loaf of bread that smells just so amazing.

Passion is enthusiasm that has you working late into the night on the "perfect" presentation.

Passion is enthusiasm that keeps you smiling, even at the end of a rough day.

Passion is what turns a job into a calling.

Passion helps you tap into your higher purpose in life.

Most of the time, when you're passionate about what you do, it doesn't feel like work. Think about your life. What do you feel passionate about? What do you love?

If you're having difficulty identifying things you're passionate about, consider your mindset.

- Do you believe in purpose?
- Do you believe you have purpose within you?
- Are you open to finding your purpose?
- Do you think finding your purpose will be difficult?
- Do you think you'll never find your purpose?

Remember, if you walk into a restaurant professing you're not hungry, chances are high you'll find nothing of interest on the menu. But, if you open your mind a little and consider that although you're not starving, you might enjoy a little indulgence. In fact, you might just find the perfect menu item to satisfy you.

The same applies to finding your passion and purpose. If you're convinced finding your passion is hard, you'll remain closed to the possibilities. You'll block out all the little thoughts, signals, and nudges. If you seek passion believing you'll never find it—guess what? **You'll never find it.** If you're not open to possibilities, those opportunities are going to pass right by you.

But if you **seek passion and purpose with an open mind, you'll find your passion and your purpose.** You'll keep an open mind about the nudges, pushes, and possibilities. You'll consider the options and see the potential. You'll explore the options and consider the possibilities. You'll grow, explore, and determine your direction. Remember, daily consistent action breeds success.

- Choose to think you can do what you love with your life.
- Choose to believe you will find your passion.
- Choose to think it **will** work.
- **Choose to think you will find your purpose.**

Take a few moments to consider:

- What are some current passions in your life?
- What are some past passions in your life?
- If you were experiencing your passions at an even deeper level, what would be going on?

COMMONALITY

> *"The commonality of the human experience is the same. We have the same sorrows, and the same triumphs. Joy is joy is joy."*

—OPRAH WINFREY

I'll ask you this again, "What do you feel passionate about?"

- What brings a smile to your face?
- What makes you happy?
- What makes you so enthusiastic you can barely contain the excitement?
- What do you enjoy reading about?
- What would you be willing to research?
- What do you remember loving when you were younger?

For each point, consider how you feel about it.

Once you identify things that bring you happiness, consider what those things have in common.

- What do the things that make you happy have in common?
- What do you love about them?
- Why do they make you happy?

Finding the commonality among our passions can help us identify the overarching ideals we value. Where our passions intersect, is important to finding our purpose. For example, a few years ago, I was getting burned out and stressed. I realized I had to reconnect with my art and what I was passionate about.

My passions were public speaking, coaching, helping people unlock their greatness, and sharing what I'd learned the hard way. What did all my passions have in common? What was my purpose? The common ground was that I needed to help others. So, I did. I reconnected to my message. I started showing people they really can have it all. I worked daily toward my goals. And it worked.

By being true to myself, I unlocked my greatness, and I'm truly happy.

That process, the journey, is what inspired me to write

this book. I live my purpose and engage my passions to create success, and now, you can too!

- Describe what your passions in life have in common.
- Describe how your passions interact and what drives them.
- Describe what drives you.

ALIGN YOUR LIFE AND PURPOSE

> *"Don't worry about what you should be doing. Ask what makes you come alive and do that, because what the world needs is people who have come alive."*
>
> —HOWARD THURMAN

Once you identify your passions, you can work toward working them into your life. You can live your passion, daily. Sometimes, all it takes is a little shift. Sometimes, a small change in how we think, perceive, or in what we believe is enough. Sometimes, that's all we need to be nudged in the right direction—our direction.

> *For me, I didn't radically change what I was doing. I did, however, make some major changes in how I was doing it. I lived my purpose.*

Whether you need to make small or big changes to make it happen, it's the same process.

1. Start by identifying your passion and purpose.
2. Then, work on getting in the right mindset to benefit from that passion and purpose.
3. Use this mindset to drive you to do daily consistent action to make it happen.

Remember, you can't do it all in one day. But, you can start today.

> *Start by identifying three things you can do to live your life with purpose while engaging your passions. Then, do those things. Work toward your progress, each and every day.*

HAVE FUN WITH YOUR PURPOSE

> *"You will receive what you ask for, no more, no less."*
> —MARK ALLEN

All work and no play makes for a very dull life. So does all play and no work. We inherently know balance is the key. But, how exactly do you find that perfect balance? First, understand it's a give-and-receive cycle.

Time is a limited resource.

For many people, the time they spend working is time

they are not able to spend playing or having fun with their family and friends.

Fun is integral to a happy life.

Study after study shows we need fun and pleasure to live happy and content lives.

When you have fun and pleasure in your life:

- You sleep better.
- You enjoy lower blood pressure.
- Your muscles relax, and tension is released.
- Your immune system enjoys a positive boost.
- You improve your blood flow, which protects you from heart disease.
- Your body releases endorphins which promote a feeling of well-being while relieving pain.
- You enjoy improved brain function.
- You feel energetic and younger.
- You burn more calories. Need I say more?

Who are we to argue with science? Taking time to have fun in our lives is important for a healthy life.

That means it's your job to have fun.

Pretty nifty idea, right? Now, get to work playing! So, how exactly do you add more fun into your life?

First, recognize and embrace spontaneous opportunities for fun.

Is your significant other looking a little smug? Fling a pillow at them and watch that smugness disappear. Of course, you might want to run right after you let the pillow fly.

- Are your kids getting a little restless? A water-gun fight always brings out the smiles and a competitive spirit.
- Is a discussion getting too serious? A (respectful) joke can lighten up the mood and change the tone of a conversation.
- Is dinner a little boring? A fun "truth or dare" session can lighten that right up.

Don't be afraid to have FUN.

Whether you plan for a weekend away, a local hiking trip, or a shopping trip, planning to have fun can bring the balance back to our lives. Game nights, nights out, and date nights can help keep your night fresh and fun.

Vacations are a prime time to engage in some serious fun.

Whether you're skydiving, cave dwelling, or enjoying a luxury spa, vacation is meant for fun. Take time to enjoy having fun.

I am always amazed at the number of people who don't take their full amount of vacation days. Seriously? Why? If you have earned the time, take it! Use it to build up your "fun account" and keep the feeling of balance in your life. There is just simply no excuse for allowing earned vacation days to go to waste. Use them and profit from the time!

Art, music, and theatre are fun.

While one person's vision of fun may be a night at an art gallery, another's may be a night at the movies. Some enjoy monster truck rallies, while others prefer a conference or listening to a guest speaker. Some want a spa day, while others may want to go dancing. Do what works for you and your loved ones.

Regardless of your vision, enjoy the night out with friends and family (with an open mind)! You never know what you'll really enjoy until you give it a chance. You might even fall in love with that latest Broadway hit.

Fun breeds more fun.

It never fails. When my family and friends get together, we invariably have the next great time planned before we split up for the night. Why? Because fun breeds fun. It's impossible not to want to experience that fun, secure, and happy feeling again. Go ahead and plan your next outing before you leave. Get it into your calendar and refuse to allow other commitments to encroach on your well-earned and well-deserved **FUN** time.

> *Think about how you have fun. List three things you can do to bring more fun into your life. Explain why this is now important to you.*

MINDSET AND EMOTIONS

....

> *"If you change the way you look at things, the things you look at change."*
>
> —WAYNE DYER

We've spent a lot of time already discussing mindset. How the right mindset can mean the difference between success and the alternative.

But, what exactly is mindset? How does it work for (or against) us?

In a **fixed mindset**, people believe their qualities (such as their intelligence or talent) are fixed and concrete. They cannot be changed and do not require any work or practice to improve. They are what they are. Of course, we know they're wrong, but some people buy into the "fixed mindset" theory. **Others know better.**

People with a growth mindset recognize they have the opportunity to continually learn and improve.

They appreciate the process as much as the outcome. A fixed mindset can wreak havoc on your self-confidence. If you expect yourself to have all the skills and abilities you'll ever need, you're going to find yourself ill-prepared for some (or most) challenges.

A growth mindset, on the other hand, encourages healthy self-confidence. You're constantly learning, improving, and working toward your goals. Part of a healthy mindset is recognizing that sometimes we need to shift to get into the right mindset.

Sometimes, we falter. Sometimes, we make mistakes. Sometimes, we miss the mark. With a growth-oriented mindset, that is not only "okay," it's great!

Recognizing we can learn from those mistakes and challenges enables us to use them to our advantage. With a growth mindset, we recognize we're constantly learning and improving. We're moving toward our ideal selves.

Just as our beliefs alter our reality, so does our mindset.

Your mindset is a filter. It helps determine how you receive and respond to information. If you're in a positive mindset, you're open and accepting, while a negative mindset can leave you closed and unapproachable. Sometimes, negative mindsets come from negative emotions, such as fear or embarrassment.

Take a moment and consider:

- What are you afraid of?
- What embarrasses you?
- What makes you angry?
- Do you have doubts?
- Do you feel regret?
- Are you resentful? Why?
- Do you feel jealousy? Over what?
- Do you feel guilty? Why?

Remember, it's okay to feel negative emotions. They are a natural occurrence.

Emotions are natural and instinctive responses to your circumstances, mood, or relationships.

You can't remove emotions from your life. But, you can shift your mindset when you're dealing with negative emotions. When you're feeling fear, self-doubt, or embarrassment, you can shift your mindset to a more positive view.

Take a moment and describe your current mindset. Ask yourself, "If I were to have more of a growth mindset, what would be different?"

RECOGNIZE HOW YOU FEEL

"When you control your thoughts and emotions, you control everything."

—MARSHALL SYLVER

Remember, emotions are natural, and they will always exist. You can't completely eliminate them. But, you can release a negative emotion and move on. How? Start by recognizing the emotion. Investigate why you feel that emotion in that moment. **Name it.**

What is the negative feeling you're experiencing?

- Are you feeling angry, frustrated, or mad?
- Are you sad or disappointed?
- Are you feeling self-doubt?
- Are you feeling guilty?
- Are you feeling conflicted or confused?
- Are you feeling hatred?
- Are you feeling envy or jealousy?
- Are you feeling hopelessness or despair?
- Are you feeling resentful or bitter?
- Are you feeling possessive or threatened?

- Are you feeling greedy, selfish, or egotistical?
- Are you feeling defeated or discouraged?
- Are you feeling isolated or judged?
- Are you feeling destructive?

Describe it. How is it making you feel? Why?

Describe how the negative emotion is affecting you and your life. Think about all the different ways this emotion is affecting you, your responses, beliefs, and actions. Consider how the negative emotion is affecting those around you, especially those you are closest to, since they often feel the brunt of your emotional outbursts first and hardest.

You can't avoid emotions, even if you want to. You need to accept how you feel and work with it. You need to identify the emotion and how the emotion is affecting you and your loved ones. Once you've recognized how you're feeling and **why** you're feeling that way, you can start to resolve the emotion.

List any negative emotions you've experienced lately.

- Why did you feel that way?
- What would you choose to feel if you were to release the negative emotions right now?

EXPRESS HOW YOU FEEL

> *"To express yourself needs a reason but expressing yourself* **IS** *the reason."*
>
> —AI WEIWEI

Once you identify the feeling, work to express it. How do you express emotion?

· How can your friends and family tell if you're upset?
· How do they know when you're sad?
· How do they know if you're feeling guilty?

Just as your family and loved ones can tell when something is wrong with you, I can always tell when a close friend of mine is angry or dealing with a frustration. Why? Because her house shines. Cleaning is one of the ways she expresses her emotions.

She works through her feelings while she's dusting, vacuuming, and scrubbing. Not a speck of dirt is left by the time she works through whatever she's feeling. **Emotions are energy.**

Emotions are full of energy. Some people physically shake when feeling strong emotions because the energy is just too much for their bodies to internalize. It must vent the excess energy, so their body shakes. My friend uses the negative emotion (anger) to generate a positive action (cleaning). She uses the energy in a constructive way. Channeling emotional energy into a constructive action not only helps her express the emotion, she benefits from a very clean house.

The alternative is to express the energy of the negative emotion in a negative way. I'm sure you know someone who does this. They may "blow up" and explode in anger. They may give in and kick or punch things. They may verbally erupt, shouting or yelling their frustration until it vents out. They're expressing their emotion in a destructive way.

Turning emotional energy into constructive work not only works off the frustration/anger/resentment—it also creates a bonus. You can look back and admire the work you've done. There are many ways to turn emotional energy into constructive results, including:

- Working out, running, hiking, swimming, or any method of physically expressing the energy.
- Cleaning and scrubbing, or organizing large projects (like the garage, basement, kitchen, or attic).
- Planting, or weeding a garden.
- Home improvement or other household projects.
- Hit or punch a pillow in your room, while you scream or cry and release any other emotions.
- Painting, drawing, sculpting, or other creative endeavors.

- Scrapbooking, looking at pictures, watching home videos, or other methods of remembering and reliving happy times.

Whether you turn to a punching bag, weeding the garden, or building a fence, use the emotional energy in a creative way and you'll move toward dismissing the emotion even quicker.

- Describe three ways you could express a negative emotion.
- What are three negative emotions you feel stuck with right now?
- Describe three ways you can express these emotions.

REWIRING EMOTIONS

> *"These mountains you are carrying, you were only supposed to climb."*
>
> —NAJWA ZEBIAN

The final step to dealing with negative emotions is to dismiss them. In other words:

- Let it go.
- Get over it.
- Move on.

But, how exactly do you do that? Remember, emotions are a natural and instinctive reaction. To rewire an emotion, you need to **respond** instead of react.

- Feeling frustrated about a situation? Change it.
- Feeling confused about something? Learn more about it.
- Feeling guilty over something? Make amends.
- Feeling embarrassed about something? Turn it around.
- Feeling afraid? Mitigate the fear.
- Feeling self-doubt? Reaffirm your positives.

No matter what emotion you're dealing with, respond with consistent positive and constructive action, and you'll soon find the negativity is dismissed.

For some, moving on might involve helping others in a similar situation. For others, it might involve generating new hobbies, or finding new activities. It may involve self-affirmations, or opportunities to build self-confidence. If you're taking daily constructive action, you're moving on.

List three ways you can "let it go" and rewire a negative emotion into a positive one.

OVERCOMING NEGATIVE SELF-TALK

> *"Brain wave tests prove that when we use positive words our 'feel good' hormones flow. Positive self-talk releases endorphins and serotonin in our brains, which then flow throughout our body, making us feel good. These neurotransmitters stop flowing when we use negative words."*
>
> —RUTH FISHEL

We are always hardest on ourselves. We know every single one of our own flaws and are often quickly willing to criticize ourselves. Why? Everyone has negative thoughts. What matters is what you do when those negative thoughts pop up.

Everyone has self-doubt.

What do you do when a negative thought pops into your mind?

- Do you take it seriously?
- Do you ignore it?
- Do you believe it?
- Do you counter it?

A single mistake doesn't wipe out a week of good deeds. In the same way, a single negative emotion won't wipe away a week of positive thinking. Repeated negative thoughts though can wreak havoc on your mindset.

When you find yourself plagued by negative and destructive thoughts, **question it.** Rethink the premise and find out if it's true or not. Is this really something you should be worried about? Is it something you should expend energy and time on? Is it something that really matters?

If you're not sure, **get some perspective.** In other words, zoom out. Will this still matter in a few days? How about a few months? Will it still be so important in a few years? If you're still being plagued by negative self-talk, consider **talking it out** with someone you trust. Once you explain your thought process and feelings, they can give you an objective perspective. Objectivity can be key to seeing something clearly.

Another way to overcome negative self-talk is to **live in the moment.** You can't worry about the future or relive the past if you're living in this exact moment. There may always be things we regret about our past. Or we may have things we wish we could change. But, ruminating on the past won't change anything.

Turn those past experiences into learning experiences and commit yourself to learning from them.

Remind yourself that you're smarter and older now, and you would act differently if you were put in the same situation again. Worrying about the future will only give you grief and anxiety. Do something constructive to combat your concern and cross it off your worry list.

How do you move things off your worry list? Let's walk through an example. Your significant other has planned your first hiking and camping trip together. Although you're very excited about getting away and hiking to the hidden waterfall, among other things on your mind, you're concerned about the wild animals you may encounter while you're hiking. Although your significant other may not share your concern, it's a valid concern. It's not irrational to you. What are some things you can do to live in the moment and move this off your worry list?

- You could research the types of animals that live in the area you'll be hiking through.
- You could use the information on the animals you're most likely to encounter to build a little safety pack. Your personal safety pack would include the things you need to feel safe on the trip. It's your personal safety net. Depending on the animals you'll encounter, your safety pack may include an emergency flare, bear spray, a snake-bite kit, or a wasp-sting kit. You may decide to pack an extra compass or an extra pair of socks.
- You could talk to other people who have completed the hike and gather information about the animals they encountered.

- You could talk to the park rangers or professionals familiar with the area and see if you need to take any special precautions, like talking loudly or not leaving food out overnight.
- Share how you feel with your partner, as expressing this emotion will help you deal with it.

There are a lot of things you could do to move your fear off your worry list. You could choose to live in the moment and enjoy the special trip your significant other planned for you. You wouldn't want to miss the beautiful cabin (with the gorgeous stone fireplace) located by the stream, next to the stunning wildflower field. Or the long walks you'll take, or the late nights together. You want to live in the moment and enjoy everything life offers. So, get to moving things off your worry list so you can live in the moment.

Describe three negative emotions you might encounter. List three ways you can deal with those emotions or mitigate your concerns, so you can live in the moment and enjoy life.

OVERCOMING FEAR

"The key to success is to focus our conscious mind on things we desire not things we fear."

—BRIAN TRACY

If you're facing fear, know you're not alone.

Everyone is afraid at some time or another.

Anyone who tells you otherwise is lying. It's that simple.

Fear is a natural and instinctive reaction to facing something potentially dangerous or painful.

When you're facing fear, consider the worst possible scenario. Ask yourself, "Realistically, what is the worst that can happen?" Let's say you're afraid of making a major change in your life—like quitting your job to go solo or moving to a new area. Imagine the worst possible realistic scenario. Then, consider the impact that would have on your life. If you can live with that scenario, you know you can survive.

So, you want to quit your day job (in retail) to pursue your passion for illustrating children's books. Consider the worst possible scenario you could realistically encounter?

What if...

Someone doesn't like your work? You could find another client or try again.

You fail to find any clients and must find another reg-

ular job in six months? Not much different than the job you have now, right?

You hate it?

Then you learned that you don't want to do that as a full-time living. That's not exactly bad news. Learning what you don't want is just as important as learning what you do want. So, if you've survived the worst-case realistic scenario, consider yourself committed. Now, you need to consider the best-case scenario.

- What if you love your new job?
- What if everyone loves your illustrations?
- What if you have so many clients that you need to hire another illustrator?

What if...

You get the idea.

> *Consider your fears. What are you really afraid of? What terrifies you or keeps you awake at night? What fears hold you back from living the life you desire?*
>
> *Take a moment and think about what truly terrifies you. Describe your fear. Ask yourself, "What is the worst-case scenario and can I handle it?"*

GROWING A POSITIVE MINDSET

> *"Life is 10% what happens to me and 90% how I react to it."*
>
> —CHARLES SWINDOLL

Growing a positive mindset is an active process. That means sometimes (but not always) you have to work at it. It doesn't always come naturally, especially when we're facing challenging situations.

A great way to improve our mindset is to focus on the things we're grateful for.

- Consider the things you love about your life. Be thankful you have them in your life to bring happiness. Even the small things help make our lives brighter and better.
- Consider your health. Be thankful you're here.
- Consider your family and friends. Be thankful for them, and for having them as a part of your life.

Consider all the good in your life, no matter how small. Take a few moments every day to be thankful for the good things.

Try practicing gratefulness throughout your day.

- Did your coworker come through in a particular

important issue? Take a moment to tell them you appreciate their hard work.

- Did your child pick up his coat (for what felt like the first time ever) without having to be told? Take the time to tell them how much you appreciate their thoughtfulness.
- Did you almost spill that cup of coffee/drop your mobile phone/have an accident? Be thankful it was a near miss!

Being thankful for even the littlest things helps us shift our mindset to a positive view. To keep a positive mindset, sometimes we need to get outside of ourselves. We need to step back and remove ourselves from our own personal situations and view the world in a larger sense.

Volunteering for a cause that's important to you is one great way to gain perspective. Whether it's people, animals, or the environment that drives you, there are lots of opportunities to give back.

Maybe you want to help coach a local youth sports team. Or maybe you'll organize a book drive, park clean-up, or other community program. Some people may volunteer for a food bank, soup kitchen, or shelter. Some may start a club, become a mentor, or practice random acts of kindness.

No matter how you do it, helping others is a great way to

refresh your mindset. Not only are we helping others, we feel better about ourselves in the process. Contributing to society gives us (and our minds) some other things to think about. We provide a reference point for our perspective and recognize our value in this world.

- Ask yourself, "If I were to have more of a positive mindset each day, what would be different?"
- Describe three things you're thankful for in your life.
- Describe one way you could step back and gain some perspective in your life by helping others.

REMOVING NEGATIVE SOURCES

> "Toxic people will pollute everything around them. Don't hesitate. Fumigate."
>
> —MANDY HALE

Sometimes, to keep a positive mindset, we need to remove negativity from our lives. If you keep running up against the same negativity in your life, consider making changes.

Are you surrounded by negative people?

If you're consistently facing negativity from specific people in your life, limit your contact with them. Reconsider what you tell them and how you confide in them. A friend of mine is an amazing writer, although she didn't always see it that way. In fact, she almost gave up writing because of some negative people in her life. When she first started out, she joined an online writer's group. She'd post each new short story and wait excitedly to read their feedback and reactions. Unfortunately, it quickly became obvious no one in the group was supportive. There was exactly one kind of feedback—negative. They'd pick apart her characters, destroy her plots, and throw every possible negative comment at her. And she kept going back for more. She thought her writing was horrible, because that's what they kept telling her.

Eventually, she gave up writing.

When her friends pushed her, she finally revealed why. Immediately, they read through her stories and realized that although they weren't all wonderful—many of them were amazing. **They encouraged her to get a second opinion.** They demanded she at least seek more information before she stopped doing something she loved.

Deciding she had nothing to lose, she sent samples of her work to five different editors, and three of the editors responded. She quickly learned that although the editors had some pointers for her, they loved her writing style. That gave her enough confidence to start writing freelance. Soon, she was being inundated with requests and was so busy she could pick and choose the writing jobs she wanted. Last year, she quit her day job and is now a full-time freelance writer. Oh yeah, she deleted her account on that writer's board, too.

Moral of the story? **Be sure you're getting honest and appropriate feedback. If you're not—look elsewhere.** Don't be afraid to get a second (or third) opinion or keep looking until you find your tribe.

- Are there any negative sources in your life?
- Describe three ways to limit or remove negative sources in your life.
- Describe how you can limit the effect of their negativity on your life.

MONEY

....

"Money is not the only answer, but it makes a difference."

—BARACK OBAMA

Most people have financial goals. Some people even have realistic and specific financial goals. What's the difference?

I want to be rich.

That is an admirable goal. But it's not very specific. It's also not realistic. Why? Because there is no way to tell when you've reached the goal.

- What does "rich" mean to you?
- When are you "rich?"
- When are you "rich" enough?

Goals (including financial goals) should be specific and achievable.

They should include specific details of what you want to accomplish. A goal should describe what success looks like.

- I want to earn 25 percent more next year than I did this year.
- I want to save 10 percent more each month.

These are solid, reasonable, and achievable goals.

Goals are relative.

While your goal may be to learn to ski, someone else's may be to excel at moguls. Your goals must take **you** into consideration. It's reasonable to expect to save an extra $50 this month, if it fits *your situation*. It's reasonable to expect to save an extra $500 this month, if it fits *your situation*.

The only goals that will work for you, need to fit you. They need to be personal, specific, and achievable.

Goals need to be measurable.

You need some way to assess and measure your results

to know you achieved your goals. In other words, put a number on it.

The goal might not always include a specific number in a specific time frame.

A savings goal may be to save more each month than the previous month. That goal works toward positive increases and success, while ensuring a gradual and reasonable method of increasing percentages saved without taxing the budget. If you have a specific number in your goal, break it down into what that means in your daily life. How do you do that?

Let's say you want to save an additional $2,000 next year. Without increasing your income, you'd need to save an additional $167 per month to achieve your goal. Or, you'd need to save $38 per week. That's just $5.48 per day.

Now, that translates into a specific activity. How do you save a little over $5 per day, or $38 per week? What could you be doing to generate an extra $5.48 a day? You could do almost anything now that you have a personalized goal, **because personal, specific, achievable, and measurable goals lead to success.**

List three specific financial goals you'd like to achieve. State the date when you want to achieve these goals.

MAKING MORE MONEY

"I'm not trying to make friends, I'm trying to make money."

—KEVIN O'LEARY

Your financial goals may include more than just saving money. You may want to **make more money.** That's certainly a common goal. But again, it's not a very specific or achievable goal.

- How much do you want to make?
- By when?
- How do you plan to do it?

When setting your financial goals, be specific, realistic, and detailed. Explain what success will look and feel like for you.

If you want to make more money, you need to consider your options.

- Will you demonstrate you deserve a raise in your current job?
- Will you pick up an additional job to increase your income?

- Will you do freelance work?
- Will you make something to sell?
- Will you join the gig economy?
- Will you change jobs?
- Will you open your own business?
- Will you sell something you own?
- Will you build revenue streams?

No matter how you decide you want to earn additional money, the first step is to set your personal, specific, attainable, and measurable goal. Then, you need to detail how you plan to make it happen.

- Describe your short-term financial goals.
- Describe your long-term financial goals.
- List three things you can do to meet your goals.

Then, do at least one of them...today.

REDUCING BAD DEBT

"Good debt is a powerful tool, but bad debt can kill you."
—ROBERT KIYOSAKI

One of the simplest ways to make your money work for you is to eliminate debt. It's pretty simple really—debt costs money.

Therefore, eliminating debt saves money.

Debt is often a burden and limits the choices we can make. Consider what you could do with the extra money you would have each month if you were completely out of debt. Working to eliminate debt helps your money work smart.

- How much do you spend on debt each month?
- How much is that each year?
- What would you do with the extra money you'd save if you paid off all your debt?

Eliminating debt is a great beginning for making your money work smarter. Develop a plan to reduce or eliminate your debt. If you have credit cards or can't eliminate all your debt, consider if you've chosen the right credit card. Of course, most credit card companies offer some type of reward or bonus system. Pretty nice of them since they're making money off your money, right? But if you never use those rewards, you're losing out on part of the value of your debt. Choosing rewards you'll use helps your money work smarter.

Many credit lenders will negotiate their credit terms if you're a current and reliable client. Try talking with your creditors to see if there is anything you can do to reduce your debt, by reducing your interest rate.

What would it mean to you to reduce your bad debt?
List two ways you can eliminate or reduce debt in
your life. Then, do one of them...today.

SAVE EARLY, SAVE OFTEN

"Do not save what is left after spending but spend what
is left after saving."

—WARREN BUFFETT

Another great way your money works for you is to start
saving early. The earlier you can start setting money
aside, the better off you'll be. If you started saving $361
per month at the age of twenty, with a return rate of 6
percent, you would have $1,000,000 dollars by the time
you retire (at age sixty-five).

But, if you wait to start saving until the age of twenty-five,
you'd have to start saving $499 per month to have the same
$1,000,000 at your retirement age. That's an extra $138
per month simply because you waited just a little longer
to start saving. If you wait until the age of thirty to start
saving, you need to save almost $700 per month, which
is almost double what you needed just a few years earlier.

The value of saving early and saving often is obvious.

Yet, there are even more benefits of saving early—compound interest. To put it simply, compound interest is your friend. Compound interest is simply interest paid on both the principal and the interest earned. In other words, your interest continues to earn interest. Let's say you save $5,000 one year and want to invest it. But, $5,000 doesn't seem like a lot of money to set aside for retirement, does it?

Well, let's see.

If you save that money in a compound interest-bearing account, you can increase the value of that savings. The longer your money is invested, the more compound interest you'll earn. For this example, we'll assume you're saving your money in an interest-bearing account, with 7 percent annual interest compounded monthly. If you saved that $5,000 when you were sixty, you'd have $7,087.99 by the age of sixty-five. Not bad, but not that great, right?

If you saved that $5,000 when you were fifty-five, you'd have $10,047.91 by the age of sixty-five. Better, but still not awesome.

If you saved that same $5,000 when you were forty-five, you'd have $20,192.09 by the age of sixty-five. Okay, now we're talking. But, $20,000 still isn't quite enough. But, if you started an account at the age of twenty with the same

$5,000, you'd have $110,596.66 by the age of sixty-five. That's assuming you don't even add to the account—ever—after you start it.

Wow. From $5,000 to over $100k just with compound interest and no additional work on your part. But remember, to create a magnitude of long-term wealth, you can't just save your way to being rich. You need to combine saving with other actions to create long-term wealth.

Starting to see the benefit of saving early and saving often?

List two goals related to saving money, or two ways you can increase your savings. Describe one financial goal you can accomplish this week.

PASSIVE INCOME

"If you don't find a way to make money while you sleep, you will work until you die."

—WARREN BUFFETT

Passive income is one of the building blocks to wealth. You certainly don't want to be trading time for money forever. Passive income is income that is earned without having to exert a lot of effort.

Passive income isn't free.

There is always an investment required, although it's not always a financial investment. For example, writing a book requires a considerable sacrifice of time and effort upfront, but little to no upfront financial capital.

There are many ways to create passive income. One example is through compound interest, which we mentioned earlier. It earns money, without additional effort on your part. Other possible passive income streams include real estate investment, silent business partnerships, websites that generate income, and others.

Examples of passive income streams include:

- Peer-to-peer lending.
- Rental property investment.
- Write and sell a book or guide.
- Create an online course.
- Develop an app.
- Create a website selling a product.
- Invest in a partnership with an existing profitable business.
- Develop an online guide.
- Create a blog and utilize affiliate marketing.
- Create a lead-capture website for real businesses.
- Build a website selling a service and outsource the work.
- Re-sell existing products.

- Purchase and rent high-end equipment or supplies.
- Earn royalties from books, songs, or other creative endeavors.

There are literally thousands of ways to earn money passively. You just need to decide which one you want to invest in. Remember, even the most lucrative passive income streams require an investment of time, money, or both to start.

How can you make passive income work for you?

List two passive income examples you would like to explore. Begin research on one of them…right now.

INVESTING

"Investing should be more like watching paint dry or watching grass grow. If you want excitement, take $800 and go to Las Vegas."

—PAUL SAMUELSON

Of course, one of the major keys to your money working smarter for you is to invest. There are too many options of where to invest your money to even consider recapping them all here. But, we'll cover the most common ways to invest money.

You can invest in real estate.

Of course, investing in real estate requires an upfront financial investment, but can generate passive income. Investing in rental properties generates income without much effort if you get it set up correctly.

You can invest in the market.

Dividend-bearing stocks, treasury inflation-protected securities, CDs, and annuities can all be part of a successful investing strategy.

You can invest in yourself.

You can spend money to improve your future earning potential. Whether that means you invest in going back to school, learning a new trade, or getting a new certification, funds spent on increasing your future earning potential are all excellent investments.

List two ways you can invest your money to make it work smarter.

REWIRING SCARCITY INTO ABUNDANCE

> *"Abundance is not something we acquire, it is something we tune in to."*
>
> —WAYNE DYER

Your thoughts are things. What you focus on, you attract into your life. If you think in terms of not having enough, guess what? You will never have enough. Change your mindset to **focus on abundance**, and that is exactly what you will get. One way to do this is to reflect on the things you already have.

The universe responds to what we focus on.

When we reflect on the things we have, the things we're grateful for, the universe responds by giving us more of those things. When we allow ourselves to feel abundant, we feel better about our lives. One of the things a lot of people fail to understand about our lives is we can have whatever we want. Once we have learned to overcome the negative thinking that keeps us trapped in a scarcity mindset, anything becomes possible. We learn that by focusing on abundance, our lives can grow abundantly, without limitation.

So, the most important step is learning to rewire our thinking around scarcity vs. abundance. Since we now know **our thoughts are things**, once we have begun to think abundantly, this mindset brings abundance into our present reality. There is no need to really think about why scarcity could or couldn't be true, since our minds take whatever we think and believe to be the truth of our own present reality.

Once we begin to do this, we eventually see the physical proof of our new abundant mindset, and from that point on, it will be impossible for anyone else, or even our own mind, to trick us into a scarcity mindset ever again. A lot of people focus on scarcity, on not having enough. It's our job though, to turn that completely on its head, so scarcity can be rewired into abundance. Make sure abundance serves something greater than yourself, and there will never be a cap on how much abundance comes into your life.

> *What would your life look like if you chose to live in total abundance? Make a note of ways in which you have been focusing on scarcity rather than abundance. Then, flip them around into a new abundant mindset.*

CAREER AND BUSINESS

....

"Great things in business are never done by one person. They are done by a team of people."

—STEVE JOBS

Work is a large part of our life. In fact, it is quite possibly the largest chunk of our time devoted to a single pursuit. Did you know you'll work an average of 98,000 hours during your life? (That's based on working 39.2 hours per week for fifty weeks each year, for fifty years of your life.)

That means almost 25 percent of your total life is spent working! And, we all know many of us work more than 39.2 hours per week, which just means we spend an even larger part of our lives working.

Since we spend so much time working, we should enjoy it, right? Wait, what? We're supposed to enjoy our work? Yes, since we spend so much time working, we should enjoy it.

Take a moment to consider that statement.

- Do you truly enjoy your work?
- Or do you tolerate it?
- Do you jump out of bed in the morning, excited to get started on your day?
- Or do you stare at the clock just waiting for it to be over?
- Do you want to be doing it for another 50,000 hours?
- Or does that thought make you tremble in horror?

I'm not saying you should love every second of every day—that's quite impossible, I believe. All work inherently has parts that require real effort, and at times are difficult. But, you should not dread going to work.

Whether you have a traditional job, a promising career, or your own business, you need to find some fulfillment in your work.

Do you? If you're not finding any fulfillment in your work, take a few moments and consider why you're doing what you do.

- Was it something you thought you'd love, but don't?
- Did it just happen and you took the opportunity?
- Did the job or company change since you started?
- Have your goals changed since you started?
- Is there another reason you're not thrilled with your work?

Where are you at currently with your career or your business? On a scale of one to ten, how much do you love it?

If your career or your business was to be in total alignment, what would be going on?

What are three action steps you can take toward this vision right now?

ALIGNMENT WITH SELF

"It is through the alignment of my body that I discovered alignment of my Mind, Self, and Intelligence."

—B.K.S. IYENGAR

A critical part of enjoying your work comes from aligning your work with who you are.

Who we are forms the basis of what makes us happy.

Think of it this way—if you're a people person and you're stuck in an office all day tied to your computer, you're probably not going to be happy.

If you're more on the introverted side, you'll probably not thrive in a position that requires constant interaction with people.

If you value the balance between life and work, you'll probably not enjoy working sixty hours a week to get ahead in a competitive business.

Your values, beliefs, interests, skills, abilities, and even your personality all factor into what you really enjoy about work (and life).

Take a few minutes and consider this question, "What would you do if you could do **anything**?

Suspend reality for just a moment and consider all the possibilities. Try to turn off the negative thinking that blocks you from thinking big. Don't limit yourself or your career—consider all possibilities.

So, what would you do if you could do *anything*?

Consider what your work would look like. What would your career look like if you had the power to make it anything you wanted? Because you do have the power to make it what you want.

You truly have the power to turn your career into what you need and want.

Want to know how to do it? **Start, by identifying what you truly want from your work.**

Sometimes, that is the hardest part, right? It might not be easy to really think about what you want, but it's definitely worth it. Remember, this isn't about what anyone else wants from you, or what you think you "should" be doing, because that won't bring you happiness.

This is only about what **you** truly want from your work. So, what do you want your workday to look like in one year? Five years? Ten years?

Visualize what you're doing on a daily basis.

- What takes up most of your time?
- How are you earning money?
- How are you defining your success?
- Are you working for someone else, or do you own your own business?
- What makes you happy about this work?
- How are you feeling fulfilled by doing that?

For some of you, you're already doing what you truly want to do. If so, congrats! It's a wonderful thing when you realize you're right where you want to be. For others, you may need to make some changes to get there. It's okay. Growth is part of life. Without growth and change, we'd be stagnant, and that's certainly not how I want to be described.

> *How do you get to the point where you're doing exactly what you want to do?*

You set goals. You work toward them daily. You never give up. You enjoy the rewards. Sound simple? It is a simple concept, but it's not always that simple to implement in our daily lives.

> *If you were to be living in total alignment with your true self, what would be going on?*

> *What is currently stopping you from living in this way?*

> *Commit to three actions that can take you toward living this way right now.*

GOALS

> *"Review your goals twice every day in order to be focused on achieving them."*
>
> —LES BROWN

Let's start with the first step—setting goals. Everyone sets goals, but not everyone achieves them. Why?

Effective goals are realistic and reasonable.

If I said I wanted to be elected President of the United States tomorrow, that would be a completely unrealistic goal. There's just no way to make that happen overnight, especially since the election isn't tomorrow! But, if I said I wanted to enter politics within one year, that would be a more reasonable goal.

If I've never held a management job, it's not reasonable to expect my next job to be in top-level management. But, it's completely reasonable to anticipate a supervisory role in my future. When writing goals, keep them reasonable, realistic, and related to your situation. Consider your experience, history, and personal situation. That doesn't mean your goals should be easy to achieve. Actually, the exact opposite is true.

You're more likely to achieve a goal that challenges you.

Studies consistently show that challenging goals are key to driving success. Your goals need to push and challenge you to make things happen. Effective goals motivate you to learn new things, develop new methods, and think differently. When a goal is challenging (but not unreasonable), it drives you to continue working and putting in the time and effort needed to make it happen.

Effective goals are detailed, specific, and exact.

Another reason some goals are not achieved is because they were not specific enough.

> *If you want to be successful, you need to identify and detail exactly what that success means to you. Success to one person may mean becoming CEO of their company, while to another it may mean financially providing for their family while having time to enjoy dinner with them each night.*

Make your goals specific and detailed, so you know exactly what you're working toward.

Effective goals are measurable.

Goals without measure are like a race without a finish line. What's the point, right? Goals need a finish line—a point where you know you achieved the goal. Without it, there is no motivation and no reason to continue to work toward your goal.

Success can be measured in both concrete and creative ways. Concrete methods of measurement are straightforward. Wanting to increase your income by 25 percent next year, provides a very concrete way to measure your success. Either you increased your income by 25 percent, or you didn't. The finish line is clear, and it's obvious if you succeed (or not).

Creative methods of measurement are not quite as straightforward, but they still have great value in measuring our success in reaching our goals.

Let's say your goal is to find more balance between work and home life. There isn't a simple concrete way to measure that and to know when you've reached your goal. That's when we turn to creative tools to measure our success.

Maybe you'd like to consider how many times you made it home for dinner. Or, maybe you could consider how often you were able to attend your son's baseball games, or your daughter's swimming meets. Maybe you count how often you carved out time last month for girl's night or poker night.

Use any metric you can to mark achievement against your

standard of success. Then (and only then), will you know you've achieved your goal.

Effective goals have a timeline attached.

A goal without a timeline attached is just a dream. While dreams are extremely important, they won't get us where we want to be. Timelines hold us accountable and keep us on track. They help us plan, organize, and work toward success.

Timelines turn goals into action.

Let's say I want to increase my savings. An admirable goal, right? Everyone wants to increase their savings, but the goal is not very specific, and it has no timeline attached.

> *There is no action inherent in the goal. There is no specific reason for me to work on it right now. It's just another dream that will float around, without any action to turn it into reality.*

If I say instead, I am going to save an extra $50 this week, that is a specific and timeline-oriented goal. It gives me a specific and exact goal tied to my actions. I must act (right away) to make it happen. It's not just a dream floating around. It will become my reality because it's specific, reasonable, and has a timeline attached.

Effective goals are directly tied to action.

Inherent in any goal is the consistent action that must occur to bring it into reality. Using the savings goal as an example: to make it reality, I need to consistently act to decrease my costs and increase my savings. That consistent, daily action is what turns a goal into reality. The best part? Daily, consistent action, compounds success. Each time you work toward your goal, the action increases.

Consistent action breeds results, which in turn, creates success.

Try to break large goals into smaller action steps. For example, if you want to start your own business, you need to break that down into the action steps necessary to make it happen.

Your action steps may include things like:

· Thinking of what kind of business you are passionate about.
· What do you need to learn about running a business?
· Create a business plan.
· Secure funding to start up your business.
· Get business coaching or advice from other people who operate successful businesses.

Action steps are the little things you need to make happen each day, to successfully reach your goals. Break goals down into the daily actions you need to take, so you can accomplish them.

After you identify the steps you need to take, take the time to **prioritize your goals.** Chances are high you'll have more than one goal at a time. Prioritizing your goals ensures you're working toward the ones that are most important to you now. Of course, that may change over time! That is one of the reasons it's so important to review and update your goals.

Sometimes the path is easy and we're able to sail toward our goals. Sometimes the path isn't easy. But it's worth it.

You will encounter barriers, roadblocks, and impediments in your quest to success.

Sometimes, we need to be flexible and adjust or modify our goals accordingly. Let's say you must work while earning that degree. It may take you a little longer than your original four years, but by adjusting the timeframe for the goal, instead of giving up, you'll accomplish it.

Don't give up on your goals if they're important to you.

However, if a particular goal is no longer important to

you, then you should consider letting it go. That allows you to place your energy into pursuing goals that are important to you.

Sometimes, what we think we want, changes, and that is okay. It's all part of that growth-oriented dynamic mindset we have as humans. When what you want changes, it just means it's time to re-evaluate and reprioritize your goals.

- What are three big goals you are committed to manifesting right now?
- How will you measure them?
- What action steps can you commit to today?

ACTION BREEDS SUCCESS

"Action is the fundamental key to all success."

—PABLO PICASSO

Once you've thought through your wants and desires, created your goal list, and know exactly what you want (and don't want), you're ready to get it. The next step is action. Take action to make your dreams a reality.

Success, in any area of your life, is a compound result of small actions taken daily.

It's true for your health, relationships, and career. Daily

and consistent action breeds success, exponentially. Take a moment and think about one of your goals. Now, break that goal into a series of actions you can take. Once you know exactly what you need to do to make it happen, consider what else you can do. Think outside the box and consider all your options.

> *What actions can you take to make that goal your reality?*

Now comes the second part of daily consistent action. **You need to do it.** You need to make the commitment to complete those actions each day to achieve your results. Remember, you can start small.

- If you want to manifest a relationship, think about what your partner would look like.
- If you want to move into that supervisory role at work, talk with your supervisor and find out what they think you need to do to make it happen. Find a mentor and discuss what they think your next step is. Join a professional group and start networking within your industry.
- If you want to release some weight, start with taking a long walk or swim. You don't have to commit to working out for an hour every day. Small and simple steps (taken consistently) will accomplish tremendous results.

- If you want to eat healthier, start with your next meal or snack. You don't have to commit to giving up ice cream (gasp!) for the entire year. Consistent, daily action will accomplish tremendous results.

Remember, even if the daily action is small, it still adds up—if you're consistent with daily action.

What are three daily and consistent actions you can commit to right now?

DESIGNING YOUR LEGACY

....

> *"All good men and women must take responsibility to create legacies that will take the next generation to a level we could only imagine."*
>
> —JIM ROHN

"It's not all about you, you know!"

How many times have you heard that? Well, you know what? It's true. Many people don't understand we aren't here to live just for ourselves. Yes, okay, living for ourselves is one aspect of our life, which includes doing the things we enjoy and achieving the things we want to achieve.

But there's a much bigger picture to life.

Those who are truly successful, those who become powerful forces for change in the world, understand they're not alone in this grand experience of life. In fact, the people who truly understand this have fully realized that to be successful, there must be cooperation and coexistence among people.

Your life is not just about you. It's about you and everyone else alive right now, and the people you'll leave behind.

If you want to be truly successful, it's important to design your legacy. Consider the people you can help with your work and with your life. Think about ways you can ensure what you do in this life leaves a lasting positive impression on others.

How can you leave behind a legacy that contributes toward the betterment of mankind? Incorporate charitable work in your business mindset. Give to those who are less fortunate than yourself. Help educate people about the very same things you are learning here.

A legacy of positive change is one that other people will adopt for themselves. It keeps the work you do in this life alive for generations, even after you leave this world behind. What better way is there to live your life, than by considering the people on this earth you can help? It's especially important when you're not here to witness it anymore.

By living like this, you'll guarantee you become the best possible kind of person you can be—a selfless person who leaves a lasting and positive contribution to mankind. As a small representative of humanity, what bigger and greater way is there to live your life? I don't know of any, and that's why contributing to our community-at-large is an essential part of what I do, and why I do it.

> *List three ways you can make greater contributions to the world with your life.*
>
> *List three ways you can ensure this continues as the legacy you leave behind.*

FAMILY AND FRIENDS

....

"Friends are the family we choose for ourselves."

—EDNA BUCHANAN

Family and friends are one of the most important aspects of life. They bring meaning and significance to our otherwise daily grind. Family is the basis for happiness and peace in our lives.

Without our family, or without harmony in our family, we can find ourselves stressed and unhappy.

So, what is family? You probably already have an answer for that. But, I'm going to challenge your language again. How do you define your family? Family isn't just those people we share DNA with.

> *Family are all the people you treat with special loyalty or intimacy.*

In other words, family isn't about blood relationships, although that can be a good beginning.

Family is about friendship, intimacy, and caring.

Family is built through a common bond of care, love, and sharing. You probably consider some people family that aren't actually blood related. Whether they've joined your family through marriage or friendship, the bonds are just as strong.

Family is based on love.

It's important to understand there are a great number of challenges involved with families.

> *In an ideal world, family will always love you—no matter what. But they might not always agree with you, and in many families, there will be personal difficulties and opposition.*

Having a commitment to your family means you will do your best to work through any issues as a collective, to find a resolution.

Family is about the people you love, and who love you equally in return. Family should protect each other.

When faced with adversity, a family should come together to form a strong unit to tackle the issue. Family should be there for us when we feel like we are losing ourselves in life. We can learn from our family. By being close to those we consider family, we are able to share and see more than we would with those with whom we are distant.

As already stated, in any relationship, there are aspects that are challenging. This is even more true with relationships involving many people at once, such as family. Since you know your family better than any other people in your life, and since they know you better than anyone else, there is more room for frustration and in some cases even neglect.

Be sure to keep the family you want to keep and disregard any family members who are toxic to your life. At the end of the day, family is just a label that we apply to those who are dearest and closest to us. You have just as much power and personal choice regarding whom you apply that label to as anything else in your life.

Choose your family wisely and ensure that they are the type of people you want to carry along with you, and the type of people you want to provide support and love for in return.

> *List three things you are deeply grateful for about your family.*

> *List three ways you can show up for your family to support them more.*

FAMILY CONFLICT

> *"Peace is not absence of conflict, it is the ability to handle conflict by peaceful means."*
>
> —RONALD REAGAN

Of course, families aren't all rainbows and sunshine. Sometimes there is dysfunction. Sometimes there are negative emotions, such as guilt, jealousy, and resentment. Sometimes there are other issues.

There is always going to be *some* conflict in families.

There are too many different personalities and perspectives for everyone to agree on everything, especially if they live together.

When facing family concerns, conflict, and negativity, seriously consider their concerns.

- Are they truly worried about you?
- Are they concerned about your future?
- Do they think you're making a wrong choice? Why?
- Have their past actions proven they're looking out for you?

If they're coming to you from a place of love and care, then chances are high they have valid concerns.

That doesn't make them right. It simply means they care. Take a moment and consider their concerns.

- Are their concerns valid?
- Have you truly considered all their points?
- Did you think through all the consequences of your choices?
- Did they bring up things you hadn't considered?
- Is there anything wrong with reconsidering your options?

Again, this certainly doesn't mean you must change your mind, but you could think things over again and be sure of your decision.

If you're still facing conflict, turn to your support system.

It's always a good idea to get a second (or a third) opinion.

Of course, you don't have to follow them! But sometimes an objective opinion can give you a different perspective of the situation.

Once you've made your choice, do not defend or justify your choices.

You can certainly explain them if you prefer, but know this, no one else needs to understand your reasons. It truly is your choice and your choice alone. You must live your life by your decisions, and you have to live with the consequences.

If you're feeling overwhelmed, get away for a few minutes and try to calm down. Being upset always makes it more difficult to work through things if you don't have a clear head.

Take a few deep breaths or think about something that makes you happy. Imagine sitting on a pristine white sand beach, hiking through the forest, or cruising around the Caribbean—anything to help take your mind away for a few minutes.

Once you've centered yourself, think about how you want to proceed from here.

Consider if there is anything you need to apologize for.

Being family doesn't make the relationship easier to navigate, or mean that you can avoid saying, "I'm sorry." In fact, the exact opposite is true. Sometimes we need to seek forgiveness from our family simply because we took them for granted, or assumed they'd always be there for us.

> *If you're facing family conflict, consider where the concern is coming from. Are they coming from a place of love?*

> *What concerns does your family have about your life? And are they valid?*

> *What steps are you taking to resolve the conflict?*

TOXIC PEOPLE

> *"People will love you. People will hate you. And none of it will have anything to do with you."*
>
> —ABRAHAM HICKS

Unfortunately, not everyone who disagrees with us does so out of a sense of responsibility or caring.

Some people just like being negative or mean. In other words, **they're toxic.**

As we know, there are toxic and negative people in

the world. People that no matter what we do, we can't please them. People that go through life expecting the worst and letting you know about it. Toxic people like to push your buttons. They know what will set you off and they use it to their advantage. While some toxic people may be unaware of how they affect others, most seem to enjoy creating chaos and disorder wherever they go. They seem to thrive on creating strife, stress, and difficulties.

Unfortunately, sharing your life with a toxic person can have long-lasting negative effects on your body, your health, and your life. High levels of long-term stress from toxic people can even cause irreversible brain damage by killing off neurons.

People who spew hatred, lies, and negativity don't have a place in our lives because we know it negatively affects us on all levels. Thankfully, there are tried and true tips available for dealing with toxic personalities.

First, stand up to bullies and insults. Refuse to allow anyone to make you feel inferior or try to belittle you. **No one can make you feel inferior without your consent.** In other words, they can't force you to feel that way. Remember that you're a good person and they are toxic. Their opinion means little because they do not come to you with good intentions.

Their goal isn't to help you—it's to make themselves feel better. Their opinions and views should be taken with a grain of salt.

You can (and should) absolutely place limits on what you're willing to accept from a toxic person.

Setting clear and explicit boundaries and limits is one of the ways to protect yourself from toxic personalities. That may mean limiting the time you spend with them, or not talking to them about specific topics. It's acceptable to refuse to discuss hot-button topics you know will light a fuse. If you know someone isn't coming to you with a good intent, you may not want to expose your vulnerabilities to them. That may mean not sharing certain aspects of your life with a toxic person.

They can't be trusted.

Stop wasting all that energy on someone you can't trust. Toxic people are draining. They drain happiness and pleasure from your life. They can drain your life if you allow it. If you find yourself in a heated discussion with a toxic person, try to rise above the situation. Don't be petty. Refuse to be dragged down to personal attacks. There is nothing to be gained from stooping to their level. Rising above their behavior is the only way to deal with it.

When discussing conflict with a toxic person, refuse to focus only on the problem. Discuss possible solutions instead. There is no point in worrying about the problem, other than trying to solve it.

Finally, don't expect someone with a toxic personality to change.

They probably won't. Of course, there is always a slim chance they will see the light and have a major life epiphany. Don't wait for it. Chances are high they will be just as toxic during your next run-in with them. Which brings us to our final option: cutting the toxic person out of your life. While this is a major step and should not be considered lightly, there are times when it is the only solution to a difficult situation.

In cases of abuse and neglect, cutting a toxic person from your life may be the only option. If that is the case, try to limit all contact and make a clean break. It's not easy, but it may be the only option to bring peace to your life. Finally, forgive them. But don't forget. Forgiveness comes from the heart and leads to emotional intelligence. It allows you to remain at peace and unburdened by their mistakes or issues. Forgiving, though, doesn't mean you forget they do not have your best interests at heart.

Are you facing any toxic people in your life? How are you going to handle their toxicity from now on?

PARENTING AND CHILDREN

"There is no such thing as a perfect parent. So just be a real one."

—SUE ATKINS

Navigating the parent-child relationship isn't easy—on either side of the equation!

Whether you're the parent, child, or both, a healthy relationship takes time, effort, and energy.

Thankfully, it has amazing rewards!

Family is of the utmost importance to young children. They depend on parents and their family to protect, teach, and support them as they grow. Their first relationships with family build the basis for how they interact with the world.

Family is the single most important influence in their lives.

Our family is there to help us grow and learn from the very first moment. They love, support, and care for us.

They help us learn to talk, walk, and love. They help us grow into our potential selves.

Family is also the foundation for the framework of our values. They're often where we learn right from wrong and form the basis of what we believe. We filter our early experiences through our family lens. As you know, your beliefs shape your reality. That means your family helps shape your reality.

It's up to you *how* that happens.

Like most relationships, the parent-child relationship changes with age. It matures, grows, and changes. Of course, it can still be stuck in the past too. Consider how much of your initial response to your family is you reacting the way they expect, or the way you have reacted in the past?

> *When was the last time you had a conflict with your parents, your family, or your child? Describe three different ways you could have responded instead.*

CONNECTING ACROSS GENERATIONS

> *"We need to remember across generations that there is as much to learn as there is to teach."*
>
> —GLORIA STEINEM

It's important to work to keep the family bond strong, no matter how far apart you are. Distance can be measured in miles and years. When families spread across generations, it's important to build bridges between the generations.

One way to connect the generations is through traditions.

Whether you build new ones or continue ones from generations past, traditions can help bring generations together. Traditions include so much more than just traditional holiday preparations. Family football games, poker nights, and family vacations can bring people of all different ages together. Cook-offs, bake-offs, and grill-offs are another great option to bring out the fun in any family.

Traditions can also include volunteering for a cause close to your heart. Nothing brings family together more than helping others, together. The shared joy and pleasure of helping builds a special bond. When young ones are involved, arts and crafts and baking are easy ways to bring generations together. So are family picnics, family reunions, and creative endeavors.

Sometimes you just need to get silly.

Consider the hilarity that will ensue at your next family

talent show! I'm sure you'll never forget grandma singing that rap song, while little Joey tap danced. Fun and silliness are sometimes the best medicine. Laughter is the concrete that holds families together.

Another way to increase the connection across generations is to encourage communication.

Whether that's a handmade card for grandpa, or a FaceTime chat with Aunt Sue, communication is key to building and keeping solid connections between generations. Possibly the most important aspect of connecting across generations is to make time for it! Just like any relationship, it requires time, energy, and enthusiasm to grow strong.

Try to set aside time for family connections.

Whether it's one dinner a week, or a visit once a month, set aside time that is only for your family. Try not to allow work and other interruptions to intrude.

> *Describe three new ways you can connect with your family. Remember, family are all the people you treat with special loyalty or intimacy. Take action on one of them right now.*

RELATIONSHIPS AND LOVE

....

> *"If you love someone, set them free. If they come back they're yours; if they don't they never were."*
>
> —RICHARD BACH

Most people think about falling in love at some point in their lives. Some even believe there is only "one true love" for them.

What if I told you we fall in love all the time. Would you believe me? It's true.

We fall in love—all the time.

We fall in love with people, places, things, and feelings. We can fall in love with a new house, car, or pet. We could fall in love with a piece of art, a new song, or a sculpture we see. We can also fall in love with ourselves. In fact, I encourage it! To truly love another, you must love yourself first. I know, I know. It sounds a little cheesy, doesn't it? But it's true.

We need to love ourselves first.

We need to fall in love with ourselves in an appreciative way, not a selfish way. Then, and only then, can we discover a source of love that doesn't run out; an unconditional and special love. It doesn't make you selfish to want to spend time on you. It makes you smart! We need to know who we are and love ourselves, so we can freely give ourselves to someone else.

You need to be comfortable with your thoughts, feelings, and quirks because they make you, **you.** You need to be comfortable spending time with yourself and your thoughts. When you learn to appreciate yourself, others can appreciate you too. So, how do you get to know yourself?

Start by meeting the real you.

Take some time to think about the person within you. It may take some time to answer these questions, but the time is well invested.

- What are you like?
- What is good about you?
- What do you enjoy?
- What are your interests?
- What have you accomplished?
- What are you passionate about?
- What are your plans for the future?
- What is interesting about you?

Trust yourself.

Understand you are trustworthy and have value. You will not hurt yourself or abandon yourself. Remind yourself to keep your own best interest in mind and work toward your full potential. Believe in your instinct and trust your gut. When you have strong feelings about something, listen to them. Don't dismiss them without giving them consideration.

Love yourself.

Can you truly say you love yourself? Completely? If you truly love yourself completely, that is wonderful. If not, take the time to fall in love with yourself again. You are capable of great love. You are worthy of that great love. Repeat that until you truly believe it.

Spend time with yourself.

Alone. Yes, alone. If that scares you, it's even more important you become comfortable with yourself.

Some ways to get to know yourself:

- Go to a movie—alone.
- Go out to eat—alone.
- Meditate quietly.
- Talk with yourself.
- Explore your beliefs.
- Journal your gratitude.
- Track your accomplishments.
- Explore your dreams and desires.

Can someone love us even if we don't love ourselves? Yes, of course, they can. **Other people may be able to see the awesomeness inside of us that we refuse to see.** Sometimes, you need to be reminded of that. When you're feeling down, people who love you can support and guide you back to a place of comfort and acceptance.

Describe your true self. Describe three ways you can get in touch with yourself and love yourself at a deeper level. Take action on one of them now.

CULTIVATING ENERGY

"Each one of us needs to discover the proper balance between the masculine and feminine energies, between the active and the receptive."

—RAVI RAVINDRA

We all have both masculine and feminine energy within us, regardless of whether we are male or female. If you think of energy as a spectrum or scale, we all fall somewhere on the scale. It's beneficial to draw on the appropriate energy when needed in our life. But it is just as important to release resistance to the energy within us.

To truly be ourselves, we need to embrace and express our masculine and feminine energies.

In today's modern world, both men and women are struggling with the challenge of expressing their gender energy in healthy ways. On one end of the masculine energy spectrum, we have the alpha-male, an ultra-aggressive and in-charge kind of man from whom power and energy exudes. He may desire power, control, and winning—at all costs.

On the other end of the masculine energy spectrum, we have the ultrafeminine and compassionate kind of man who may waffle indecisively. He lacks power, control, and rarely wins—at anything.

Unfortunately, either end of the spectrum is an unbalanced and unhealthy perception of our energy.

While the ultra-aggressive man is compensating for not being with his feminine energy, the ultra-feminine man is compensating for not balancing his masculine energy. Since we all have both energies within, it's important to balance them and use them to our advantage when we need or want them.

So, how do we balance these competing energies?

By engaging both kinds of energy regularly, we can balance our energy levels and use them to our advantage. A person with balanced energy is independent and in control. They take responsibility for meeting their own needs and understand no one owes them anything. Of course, they share meaningful relationships with other men and women, but they recognize these experiences add to their life, not make it. There are many ways to engage your masculine or feminine energy.

> *Describe where you feel you fall on the scale of masculine and feminine energy. Remember, you have both within you, and both have true value in our lives.*

> *Where do you want to be on the scale of masculine and feminine energy?*

How would this change make your life different?

MASCULINE ENERGY

"The masculine energy was about survival. The male was the hunter who risked his life and had to be in the fight/ flight mode."

—DEEPAK CHOPRA

Certain activities encourage your masculine energy to thrive more than others. By encouraging your masculine energy to grow, you will feel increased drive and focus. You'll find yourself with an improved libido and will overcome challenges easily. The most obvious way to engage your masculine power is to pursue the masculine relationships and activities in your life. In other words, go do something with the men you know.

Something magical happens when you are exclusively in the company of masculine energy.

You soak it up and inspire more masculine energy to come through. If you feel like your masculine batteries need recharging, hanging out in the company of men will do wonders for you.

Just a few ideas for chilling with the guys include:

- Compete in a game of basketball, football, or other sport.
- Bet on a game of pool.
- Explore a new city together.
- Get tickets to a sports game.

Another way to engage your masculine power is to practice manly habits and hobbies. Cultivate your masculine energy through traditionally male activities, such as:

- Lifting weights.
- Competitive sports.
- Martial arts.
- Outdoor adventure.
- Extreme sports.
- Fishing or hunting.

An intense workout of heavy weight or challenging exercises will quickly bring out your masculine energy.

Vigorous exercise gives you an endorphin rush, a boost of testosterone production, and allows you to sweat out all your stresses. It's good for your health, sex drive, and self-esteem. Fighting (in a safe and controlled environment) brings out a rush of testosterone—the aggression hormone.

Everyone should know basic self-defense. Taking martial arts or self-defense classes builds confidence and energizes your masculine energy. Martial arts, boxing, and kickboxing are all good options for building masculine energy. Another option is shadow boxing, where you throw punches at an imaginary opponent. Exercises that cultivate masculine energy are often regimented, focused, and disciplined. These things will get you in touch with your natural strength, independence, and manliness.

Another way to build masculine energy is to take on difficult challenges.

Trying to beat a challenge (even without winning) will build self-confidence and masculine energy. So, set goals, and run after them. Whether you succeed or not is secondary to the fact you went after them with all you've got. Being decisive also builds masculine energy. Decisiveness is key to success and inner peace. When you are decisive, you meet your goals much quicker, which provides structure to your life.

Masculine energy is also built by being action-oriented.

Take inspired actions toward your goals. Each time you work toward that goal with action, you're building your masculine energy. What actions will bring you closer to your dreams? What actions can you take today to make yourself happier?

> *Describe three ways you can get in touch with your masculine energy. Then, commit to doing one of these right now.*

FEMININE ENERGY

> *"Individually and collectively, we are shifting from a position of fear into surrender and trust of the intuitive. The power of the feminine energy is on the rise in our world.*
>
> —SHAKTI GAWAIN

Certain activities encourage your feminine energy to thrive more than others.

Feminine energy is moving energy, always changing and shifting, constantly in motion.

To encourage your feminine energy, keep moving. Whether that means a walk on the beach, a yoga class, or dancing the night away, feminine energy is activated by movement. Because feminine energy is motion and movement, it doesn't like to be boxed in. If you are female, you should know that jeans and pants can restrict your feminine energy. Try wearing skirts and dresses for a while to encourage your feminine energy. If you are male, try wearing shorts to give you greater freedom and flow of energy around your legs.

Spending intentional time with women encourages your feminine energy.

Feminine energy connects through verbal communication. It's no secret women are more verbal than men. So, it shouldn't come as any surprise that feminine energy is more verbal too. The feminine in you is nourished by extended catch-up sessions with loved ones and friends. So, take time to stay connected and keep in touch. While masculine energy can get lost in thought, feminine energy can get lost in the senses.

To connect with your feminine energy, indulge your senses. That may mean indulging in amazing food, a sensual shopping trip, or gorging on the sights and sounds of your daily life.

Feminine energy is creative.

Painting, writing, singing, and even cooking builds feminine energy through creativity. We need both masculine and feminine energy within ourselves to fully connect with our potential.

Describe three ways you can get in touch with your

feminine energy. Why do you need both masculine and feminine power in your life?

ATTRACTING YOUR IDEAL PARTNER

"...one can't avoid the storms and calamities of life, but one can at least find the right partner to face them with."

—LISA KLEYPAS

You may have a list of qualities you're searching for, or you may have absolutely no idea what you're looking for. But like anything else in life, you won't get what you want unless you specify what you want.

What do you want in a partner, significant other, or intimate relationship?

Make a list of the characteristics your ideal partner would possess. Remember, thoughts are things. You create your reality, including your partner. Include in your list what qualities you want your partner to possess. Each person's list will differ. Some may write about how they want their partner to look, while someone else may describe their personality. Describe any other traits you'd like your life partner to possess. You may also want to describe the kind of job they have and where they live—or not. It's up to you to decide what is important in your list.

Be specific about what you want, and what you don't want.

Take a few minutes to detail what you're looking for in your ideal partner. What will your life look like once you've manifested this ideal partner?

DEAL BREAKERS

"Adultery is the ultimate deal breaker for me. I would rather be alone than in a relationship that doesn't honor me."

—GARCELLE BEAUVAIS

While some things on your list can be negotiable, you should also include a few deal breakers. Deal breakers are things you feel so strongly about, they could potentially cause a problem in your future relationship. For example, if you know you absolutely want kids, it doesn't make sense to plan a future with someone who doesn't. Or vice versa. Don't go into a relationship with the plan to change the other person over to your wants. It's a recipe for disaster and will end in someone (or more than one person) getting hurt.

Think about the conditions that would make you consider ending a relationship. Deal breakers are things you're just not willing to deal with in a serious relationship.

Every person's deal breakers will be different, and that is okay.

Some examples of serious relationship deal breakers could include:

- Anger issues.
- Abuse.
- Alcohol or drug problems.
- Already in a committed relationship or married.
- Untrustworthiness, lying, or cheating.
- Laziness.
- Manipulative.
- Narcissistic behavior.
- Conflicting views on having children.
- Desiring an obedient partner.
- Flirting with other people while on a date.
- Neglecting a relationship.
- Passive-aggressive behavior.
- Lack of sexual compatibility.
- Insulting or degrading comments.

These are just some of the deal breakers people have identified in their relationships.

Describe your non-negotiable deal breakers that would prohibit a relationship from continuing. Where have you not committed to these deal breakers in the past, and what effect has that had on you?

DEFINING THE RELATIONSHIP

> *"Definition is the companion of clarity; clarity is the guide to your goals."*

> —TONY BUZAN

It's just as important to be clear about what you need and want from your relationship goals as it is with everything else in your life. Defining your relationship means you have a clear idea of exactly what you want from your partner, from yourself, and includes the specific details of your relationship.

These can include details about a potential future family, money, living arrangements, work situations, amount of time spent together or apart, your partner's family and background, etc.

Think about what you want all these aspects to entail. Then, describe what your ideal relationship is like.

- Imagine talking to them. What are you talking about?
- Where are you? When do you spend time together?
- How do they treat you on a daily basis?
- What is important to them?
- What do they smell like?
- How do you feel when you're around them?
- What do you both laugh about?
- What do you enjoy doing together?

- What do you love about them?
- What do you create and work on together?
- How do you grow together?

No matter how you describe your ideal partner, the most important aspect of attracting your ideal partner is believing they can be yours.

You need to truly believe you are worthy of their love.

You need to truly believe you deserve to have them in your life. You need to truly believe you **will** have them in your life. Self-confidence is crucial to attracting love into your life. Believing you are lovable, deserving, and worthy is one of the major ways of achieving these very things. To open yourself up to the possibility of love, you need to take some risks and go outside your comfort zone.

You'll be vulnerable. Be courageous and let go of your insecurities. Remember you are worthy, valuable, and you deserve this love. Open yourself up to new situations and possibilities. Meet new people, go out on dates, and wade through early relationships until you find your ideal mate. If you're rejected along the way, don't take it personally! Everything is not a personal rejection, so don't let rejection bring you down. Be in the moment, have fun, and believe you'll find your ideal partner!

Now, detail what your ideal relationship looks and feels like. What will that relationship add to your life? Who do you need to be to attract that kind of relationship?

GROWING LOVE AND RESPECT

"Our love is sharpened by the stone of our challenges and strengthened by the struggles of our growth."

—STEVE MARABOLI

Once you've found your special love, how do you ensure you'll grow together in love and respect? So many relationships fail and end in divorce, it's scary.

How do you ensure your relationship will succeed in love?

First, understand every relationship requires work. You must be willing to commit the needed time and energy to build a successful relationship. Yes, relationships take work. No, they're not always easy. Relationships require time and effort to grow. **That means you need to make it a priority.** If it's truly important to you, your relationship will be a top focus of your time and efforts.

To build a successful relationship, take an interest in your partner's interests.

If they love golf, watch it with them or go play a round. If they enjoy water skiing, try it out or go in the boat while your partner skis. Take time to share in what your partner loves, and they'll love you for it.

▌ *Of course, that's assuming you really want to be there.*

There is no point in pretending to go along, just to huff and puff when it's not your thing. You need to keep an open mind and be open to the possibility that even though you may not love the activity, you love your partner enough to enjoy going with them.

Be vocal and demonstrative in your love.

In other words, tell them you love them and show them you love them. Acknowledging your love encourages it to grow and encourages you to be thankful for your partner and their love. We all know actions speak louder than words, so don't just tell them you love them—show them!

Take the time and make the effort to do special things for them.

Whether it's bringing them their favorite coffee during a rough day, or dropping by with lunch, show them you care.

Communicate with your partner.

Open, honest, and sincere communication is part of every healthy relationship. Important conversations shouldn't be put off, but neither should they be initiated during awkward or inappropriate times. Be considerate of your partner and their needs and bring up discussions when you're both at ease. Deep conversations require deep listening. Make time for both of you to share with each other.

Listen and hear them.

Take the time to listen, hear, and understand what your partner needs from you and your life together. Then, support them in making it happen.

When you love someone, you give up the right to be right.

It doesn't matter who is right and who is wrong, because when that is all you concentrate on, no one wins. Least of all love. Take the time to recognize no one has to be right. You both will lose (in the long run) if there is always a winner.

Love unconditionally.

Don't place conditions and expectations on your love. That doesn't mean you shouldn't expect certain things from your partner, because you should. It simply means love them no matter what.

- Love them when they make a mistake.
- Love them when they're down and feeling vulnerable.
- Love them when they're feeling up and confident.
- Love them when they're mad or unreasonable. Or you are.
- Love them when they're hurting. Or you're hurting.
- Love them when they're wrong. Or right.
- Love them always, and forever.

Make time for each other—consistently.

No relationship can survive and thrive without time and attention. Be sure you're giving your relationship the time it needs to thrive. Find and make time for your partner and their needs. Commit to going out often and regularly. Making time for each other is important in a relationship.

For some partners, this equates to a regular date night. For others, it means spontaneous nights away or day trips.

Don't let your relationship slide by without making time for each other.

Even science backs this up. According to a study by the National Marriage Project at the University of Virginia, married couples who date each other at least once a week are three times as likely to be satisfied in love. They're also half as likely to consider divorce. Definitely a positive reason for date night!

Being there for your partner means you're truly there in the moment for them. Don't let work, pressures, and other parts of life interfere with your relationship. Turn off the work phone, limit the sports talk, and connect with your partner.

That means focusing on and listening to your partner.

It means working with them, not against them. And it definitely means putting down all electronic devices during dates. To truly be there, you need to be present in the moment.

A lot of couples want romance in their relationship.

Luckily, being romantic is as simple as being thoughtful. For example, write a short note to your partner before leaving for work. Or, drop off an unexpected lunch for them and their co-workers. Pick up the groceries or clean the bathroom. Drop off the dry cleaning or make the coffee. Feed the dog or walk the dog.

Do something unexpected for your loved one.

Doing something unexpected for your partner is romantic and thoughtful. These romantic gestures remind your partner you're thinking about them and love them.

> *What would be different if you were to love and respect your partner at a deeper level? Describe three ways you can grow love and respect in your relationship. Then, commit to doing one of them today.*

HEALING THE RELATIONSHIP WITH YOURSELF

> *"Perhaps, we should love ourselves so fiercely, that when others see us they know exactly how it should be done."*
>
> —RUDY FRANCISCO

The most important relationship in your life is the one you are having right now with yourself. Though everyone else can come and go in your life, you can always guarantee that you will have yourself for company. Knowing yourself deeply is one of the most important things you can aspire to do in this life. When you understand your strengths and weaknesses, your flaws and imperfections, your nature and your capacity, you can live a life that reflects upon and improves upon who you really are.

You must take time to consider the deep questions about yourself and your life.

There is too much room for disharmony in our minds. It

is too easy to get down on ourselves, to think negatively about ourselves, and lose sight of the truly amazing person we can be. Our relationship with ourselves is the number one priority when we want to live the kind of life that's unlimited and inspired.

If we don't love ourselves, how can we ever expect other people to love us?

If we aren't kind, compassionate, understanding, and knowledgeable about our own nature, how can we ever hope to offer the same qualities to other people? Or even require others to offer them to us?

Inner healing can only take place when we have real and deep love for ourselves.

Being with ourselves fully can help us achieve this higher state of mind. Spending time alone can help us recognize this person we've been for the duration of our lives.

By understanding the things we're afraid of, we can figure out how to grow and develop the kind of unlimited potential we want to have. What good would it do to learn about and do all the things that life has to offer, if we take our own self for granted? Or neglect ourselves to the point of self-hate and self-destruction? This is far more common than you might initially think.

Take some time out to be by yourself and reflect deeply on the issues you have not yet resolved within your mind. Make a note of these and work out some ways you can set about creating a positive change. What is one thing you can do right now to love yourself at a deeper level?

TAPPING INTO YOUR SEXUAL ENERGY

"It is sexual energy which governs the structure of human feeling and thinking."

—WILHELM REICH

You are a sexual being! There is no denying that fact. Even those of you who haven't had much experience with intimacy, you have still experienced the raw and unharnessed power of your sexuality.

How? In the form of your desire!

Your desire is the key to your power in life. Your desire is driven by your sexual energy. Sexual energy is creation energy.

When you desire something, your brain releases chemicals that push you closer to the thing you desire, even if that only means it possesses your thoughts for a while. To master our destiny, we must learn to tap into and harness this raw power. Of course, this can be utilized in a sexual way. We can develop greater capacity for sexual expression by cultivating this sexual energy. But this isn't the only way sexual energy can be applied.

Through exercises that stimulate sexual energy, we can use it to focus our minds to achieve the results we want to see.

As an exercise, think about something you desire sexually.

This can be a person, or it can even be something you fantasize about in a sexual way. Notice how immediately there are changes in your body. Your energy levels increase, and there is increased blood flow in certain areas of your body. What you have just done here is activated your sexual energy.

Now, think about something else you desire in your life, something not related to sexuality.

The energy you first manifested with your sexual thoughts now goes into the new thing you are thinking about. This is extremely powerful at manifesting things in your life. In fact, it is an old form of spiritual cultivation that meditators have used for thousands of years.

When sexual energy is cultivated and not spent, the meditator can use this ability to heal themselves and even other people. It can also bring about spiritual awakening and mystical experiences. You can use your sexual energy to hone in and focus your mind on the things you want to change.

Be careful with this one. Unguided sexual energy is like a ticking time bomb. **Make sure your life is balanced enough so you spend enough energy throughout the day.** If you find yourself getting a little agitated, stop cultivating for a while and do something to spend the excess energy you've gathered.

> *How connected to your sexual energy are you on a scale of one to ten?*
>
> *What would be different if you were more connected to your sexual energy on a daily basis?*
>
> *What are three different ways you can tap deeper into your sexual energy right now?*

SEXUAL HEALING

> *"Nothing ever goes away, until it has taught us what we need to know."*
>
> —PEMA CHODRON

For some people, it may be necessary to dive into a journey of sexual healing. Believe it or not, many people actually experience varying degrees of trauma in relation to sex. This could either be from negative experiences when first exploring sexuality, or from situations of abuse they experienced at certain times. These are extremely sensitive issues and must be approached with great wisdom and compassion.

There are a few things you can do, if you feel you need to experience some kind of healing in your life due to sexual trauma.

- **Talk about it**. If you can muster the courage to talk about what happened with a professional, you will find this releases the burden you carry. They can also help with techniques to overcome it.
- **Discuss things with your partner.** By discussing your experiences with your partner, and talking about your fears, you can work together to slowly reintegrate sexuality into your life, in the way you want it to be.
- **Personal reflection/introspection.** Sometimes the trauma that is being held in your mind can be the result of an old negative or destructive mindset. If this is the case, a good dose of self-reflection can help reveal where things need to change. This is not the case with most sexual traumas, but it can sometimes be the underlying issue.

- **Slowly become sexual again.** If you have the right kind of partner who you can take things slowly with, it may just be a case of needing to slowly get back into the swing of things regarding your sexuality. Think about easing yourself into a hot bath or getting back on a horse that you fell off of. Just take your time and start with small steps. After a while, you might find your internal state changes due to the new exposure, where you begin to feel more capable of handling your need for sexual expression.

If you have experienced sexual trauma in the past, write a note to yourself about what you have experienced, and how it is limiting your life now.

If you have a partner, sit and discuss it with them, and express that you would like to encourage sexual healing.

Practice one or two ways in which healing can occur, and also consider traditional therapy either alone or with your loved one.

SPIRITUALITY

....

> *"People take different roads to seeking fulfillment and happiness. Just because they're not on your road does not mean they are lost."*
>
> —DALAI LAMA

Spirituality means something different to everyone. But, spirituality is important to every human, even if they are skeptics.

> *Spirituality is being concerned with the human spirit or soul. It may include a sense of connection to something bigger than ourselves or the search for meaning in life.*

For some people, spirituality is expressed through participating in an organized religion.

Going to a church, synagogue, or mosque and the traditions associated form the basis for their spiritual journey.

For others, it's more personal.

It may be about getting in touch with their spiritual side through meditation, yoga, or reflection. Or, it may involve communing with nature or through the creative arts. According to scientific research, even people who claim they aren't religious or spiritual still have a sense of being connected to a greater purpose.

We naturally look for patterns and reasons within the chaos of our world, and then seek meaning from those patterns. Meaning may come from religion and/or spiritual or personal beliefs. While spirituality may incorporate elements of religion, it is generally broader than a single religion.

Questions regarding your spirituality may include:

- Where do I find meaning in my life?
- How do I feel connected to the larger world around me?
- How should I live my life?

Spirituality is about seeking a meaningful connection with something larger than ourselves. This connection results in positive emotions such as peace, contentment, gratitude, and acceptance.

Questions regarding religion may include:

- What practices, traditions, and rites should I follow?
- What is true in my beliefs?
- What is right and wrong?

Take a moment and write down what spirituality means to you. Ask yourself, "If I were to deepen my spiritual journey, what would be going on?"

FINDING PEACE

"You'll never find peace of mind, until you listen to your heart."

—GEORGE MICHAEL

Some people think being at peace means you'll feel happy all the time. Being at peace is not the same thing as being happy.

Peace is quiet and tranquility. It's freedom from disturbance.

Peace is a state of mind. It doesn't come from external things. It's within us. To be free from internal disturbance, we need to take time to allow peace to enter our lives. We need to escape the disharmony and noise of the world.

Peace means we are in harmony with ourselves and our world.

Science says it takes twelve minutes of quiet for cortisol (the stress hormone) levels to drop when stressed. Even science agrees we need quiet time to gain peace.

To find peace, we need to take time to allow ourselves to settle.

Outside distractions prevent us from concentrating within ourselves, where we can find peace.

Some people find peace through meditation.

Meditation involves thinking deeply or focusing clearly. Meditation involves turning your attention to a single point of reference. Some people focus on their breathing while others focus on bodily sensations. Some people chant a mantra or phrase while meditating. Meditation involves turning your attention inward and concentrating on the present moment. While meditation doesn't always bring peace in the moment, it's an important step of finding peace in your life.

Finding and maintaining peace in your life is a journey.

It's not about the destination, because there is no endpoint. It isn't about the result. It's about the process. To gain the most from your life, take time to find your harmony and peace, and to reflect on you and your life.

Describe three ways you can work toward having more peace in your life.

VALUES AND PEACE

"When your values are clear to you, making decisions becomes easier."

—ROY E. DISNEY

Finding peace involves eliminating distractions.

That may mean removing clutter or removing complications from our lives. For others, it may mean simplifying their lives to encourage peace. To find peace, some people need to cut down on their external commitments and eliminate extra things they take on. Remember, peace takes time. Freeing up time to spend focusing on our internal mind is an important part of finding—and maintaining—peace. That means we may have to slow things down in our lives to encourage peace to enter. If we're so busy we don't have time to breathe, we can't expect to find peace.

Eliminating extraneous commitments starts with prioritizing your values.

When we take the time to figure out what is truly important to us, it makes it easier to determine what stays on our list and what goes. Knowing what is truly important to you and your life allows you to align your life with those values. For example, if you value family time and need that connection with your loved ones to find peace, then you probably won't find peace in a career that involves years of long hours.

That doesn't mean certain occupations are off limits. But, it may affect how we implement that career in our lives. For example, if you place high value on family time and want to be a lawyer, you may find a better match in a smaller office than in going for partner in a larger firm.

Determining your values and prioritizing them is integral to determining what breeds your peace. Some values to consider include:

- Accountability and responsibility
- Achievement and ambition

- Adventure and exploration
- Balance in work and life
- Belonging and acceptance
- Community and helping society
- Compassion and caring
- Consistency and reliability
- Control and power
- Creativity and curiosity
- Enthusiasm and excitement
- Equality, diversity, and tolerance
- Fairness and justice
- Faith and spirituality
- Fun and enjoyment
- Health, well-being, and fitness
- Honesty, honor, and integrity
- Independence and self-reliance
- Leadership and command
- Mastery and perfection
- Positivity and optimism
- Security and stability
- Simplicity and clarity
- Thankfulness and gratitude
- Truth-seeking and authenticity
- Uniqueness and originality

Remember, prioritizing our values is integral to breeding peace and harmony in our life. Taking time to figure out what is truly important to us makes it easier to focus on the most important things in our life. This aligns your life to your values.

Take a moment and prioritize your top five values. Try to keep it to five or less—if everything is a top value, then nothing is truly important.

MAINTAINING PEACE

"Ego says, 'Once everything falls into place, then I'll find peace.' Spirit says, 'Find your peace, and then everything will fall into place.'"

—MARIANNE WILLIAMSON

Living your life with harmony according to your values breeds peace.

Part of living a peaceful life is understanding you won't have all the answers—ever. There are always going to be times when you should look beyond yourself for answers.

And even then, you won't always find them. That's not a bad thing—it's just part of our life. Recognizing there will be times when you're not sure what the best answer is, feels freeing. Being free of the responsibility of always knowing what to do allows us to explore all our options. Be free to consider any and all possibilities.

Part of finding peace is recognizing your achievements.

Take note of your progress and appreciate when you do well. Take a moment and offer gratitude for doing well and being in a good place. Take a moment to pat yourself on the back for a job well done. When things don't go well, remember, no one is perfect. Perfection does not exist within humans, and the quicker we can accept that, the quicker we can move toward peace.

Finding peace involves practicing patience and accepting things don't (and won't) always follow our timeline.

You can't force certain things to happen, no matter how much you want to. We should accept that some things are simply out of our control. **Once we accept that, we can move toward peace and acceptance.** Peace is a state of heightened awareness, where we are more conscious of ourselves and our choices. This requires an awareness of the thoughts that constantly flow through our mind. That means we need to catch (and eventually eliminate) all the excuses, regrets, and recriminations we live with. There are going to be things we regret about our past selves. Learning to accept and live with our choices allows us to find peace in the current moment.

That means accepting ourselves and others even with our imperfections.

Being tolerant of others and yourself is about appreciating diversity and differences. It's about being willing to live and let live, even when we disagree. Forgive yourself and others for past choices and the consequences of those choices.

We need to think long term rather than short term to encourage peace in our lives. Working toward our ideal selves is a long-term proposition. It takes time, energy, and learning to live up to our ideal potential. Finding peace doesn't mean life will be all roses and rainbows.

Even within peace, there is pain.

But with peace we can work through the pain to find a place where we are in harmony with our inner selves.

> *What would your life look like if you were more committed to creating peace in your life? Now, consider ways in which you avoid peace. Take a moment and consider how you will now allow peace to enter into your life.*

FINDING HAPPINESS

> *"Happiness is letting go of what you think your life is supposed to look like and enjoying everything that it is."*
>
> —MANDY HALE

Happiness is simply the state of being happy. But happiness is a transient quality that comes and goes.

So, how do we maintain happiness in our lives?

First, understand only part of happiness is controllable. According to research, about 40 percent of our happiness is under our control. The other 60 percent is predetermined by biology and recent life events. We are all born with a natural temperament and some people have a natural tendency to be happier than others. Thankfully, we have control of our thoughts, and we understand our thoughts create our reality. That alone gives us a leg up in the quest for happiness. If you create your reality, then you create your happiness. How you react and respond to your daily life is completely in your control.

Take the time to savor your daily experiences.

Pause to delight in the smell of a flower or take time to enjoy the wonderful sight of a hummingbird hovering in the air. Take time to enjoy the world around us, as it brings happiness into our lives.

Events affect our happiness, but the effect diminishes over time.

Think about the last big thing you bought. At the time, you were probably very excited and happy to purchase it.

How do you feel about it now?

Material purchases may bring a short-term boost in happiness, but it rarely lasts. What was novel and exciting yesterday is just the new normal today. It loses its value when it loses its newness.

Thankfully, other things can bring lasting happiness to our lives.

Quality relationships make us happier. The connection with other people, caring for and about them, and sharing our lives with them increases our happiness.

Happy people are also more successful, so happiness breeds success.

Thankfully, there are lots of ways to increase our happiness quotient. Meaningful activities also breed happiness. Research shows giving and helping others makes the giver feel happier. It can also help you be more grateful about what you have when you encounter less fortunate people.

Practicing gratitude increases happiness.

As we appreciate what we have and are thankful for it, we bring happiness into our lives. Research shows thankfulness can also improve your health and mood.

Releasing negativity increases happiness.

Find a more optimistic viewpoint and hold onto it. Try to look at your strengths and achievements rather than your mistakes. Focus on the positives of a situation rather than the negatives.

Learning new things can increase happiness as it expands our awareness.

We discover new ways of expressing ourselves and interacting with our world.

Research shows fresh air and sunshine increase our happiness levels, so get outside when you can.

Take a short walk through the park or sit and enjoy the sun shining on your face. Take a weekend away to enjoy the beach or your favorite nature spot. Connecting with nature increases our happiness and decreases our stress levels—a win-win for us all!

What would living a happier life mean to you?
Describe three ways you can increase happiness in
your life. Now, do one of them today.

CONNECTING TO SOURCE

"Your work is to go forth into this physical environment
looking for things that are a vibrational match to joy,
connecting to Source Energy, and then following with
the inspired action."

—ABRAHAM HICKS

You have a connection to an infinite resource, the Source. Some people call this "God," some people call this "Buddha," and some people call this "Mind" or "Consciousness," but whatever label you give it, we are talking about the same thing. The Source of all creation is within you. You don't need to seek for it, you don't need to travel to find it, and no one else can reveal its wonder to you.

To connect with Source, all you have to do is quiet your mind, look within, and listen for that ancient and powerful wisdom that springs up spontaneously from inside. It has never left your side, and it can never be depleted. More and more people are awakening to this amazing and life-changing power. There are ancient schools of philosophy and meditation that even teach people how to reawaken their connection to it.

It serves as an infinite resource for compassion, understanding, creativity, inner peace, joy, wisdom, and love.

The reason there is so much violence and conflict in the world today is because many people have forgotten they share a connection to this timeless and ageless wonder. One of my biggest passions is helping people remember their connection, so we can begin to explore and live a way of life that's more in tune with positivity and love, rather than negativity and hatred.

One of the quickest and most powerful ways to reawaken your connection is to learn how to meditate.

When we meditate, our thoughts are given space to settle, and we begin to sense an overwhelming feeling of joy and inner peace. From here, we are more able to directly see and feel our connection to the things around us. We are also able to more clearly see how it is us who dictates the outcome of our lives, by the contents of our minds and things we focus on.

Our thoughts are things, remember?

I truly consider meditation to be an essential life skill. I know I wouldn't have gotten where I am without it. The most basic practice of meditation is to sit and be aware of your breath. You start by putting yourself somewhere comfortable and without any distractions going on around you. You can sit, stand, lay down, or even walk, if you prefer that. Breathe naturally and calmly.

Your mind may wander, but if it does, just let go of the thoughts and return your attention to your breath.

If it helps you to focus, you can count your breaths, but when you reach ten without getting distracted, you can stop counting and simply breathe consciously. I won't go into too much detail on what to expect or where to go from here, but I will say you should delve as deep as you can into meditation. The benefits are endless, and when you do manage to reawaken your connection to Source, everything in your life will make sense. You will feel as though you have a brand-new lease on life.

List at least three times in your week where you can practice some meditation and being still.

Make a note of the things you experience while meditating.

If there are difficulties, pay special attention to these and commit yourself even more to conquering them.

When good things start to happen, celebrate! You are reawakening your connection to Source!

BECOMING AVAILABLE

"When you contact the Higher Self, the source of power within, you tap into a reservoir of infinite power."

—DEEPAK CHOPRA

A closed mind is a prison that too many people are confined by. An open mind is a limitless resource for love, joy, wonder, and compassion. Open your heart to the possibilities that life presents, and you will be carried away by the infinite ocean of creation and exploration. To become our best self, we must allow ourselves to be open to Source.

By being available to Source, we are better able to recognize the signs we are given regarding what choices to make and what things to focus on in life. Source takes into account our needs and the needs of others and helps us all to manifest them. It's a universal resource for positive change. It is the intelligence of life that gets behind us to support what we do.

Practice being available to Source throughout your daily life.

You can do this by paying close attention to what happens

around you and within you. Look for signs, push-pulls, nudges, things that are manifesting in your field of awareness. Source is always looking to guide you, but it cannot do that unless you are available. If you pay close enough attention, you will begin to understand the very subtle ways in which Source communicates with us and guides us. This is a very powerful key to the abundance mindset we spoke about earlier. While this will definitely do amazing things for your own life, the other people you help with this will also be infinitely grateful, thereby strengthening their own connection to Source.

By its very nature, Source is infinite and completely positive.

When you live a life connected to Source, your life will overflow with opportunities to make the world a better place. You will experience the many joys and wonders that life holds inherent. When you know you are genuinely working with Source, you are guaranteed to succeed and more of the people you meet and work with will have access to this truly amazing and abundant resource.

This is one of the most powerful forms of "living positively" that I have discovered, and it comes highly recommended.

Make a note to pay very special attention to the things that appear in your environment throughout the day, because this is where Source communicates with you.

Write down any ways you suspect Source is communicating with you and describe what you think it is trying to tell you. List the ways you can take the action that Source wants you to take, and then take them.

CONTRIBUTION
AND IMPACT

....

> *"Only those who have learned the power of sincere and selfless contribution experience life's deepest joy: true fulfillment."*
>
> —TONY ROBBINS

This is all about living beyond yourself. What does that mean? It means recognizing the fact **you are a single human being in the collective society of humanity.** It means considering **what you can do to make the world a better place.**

The most memorable people who have ever lived all made some sort of lasting contribution that influenced the outcome of human evolution. Yes, there are some negative examples, but we're going to stay focused on the positive now, aren't we? By living in a way that contributes positively to our social lives and environment, we are literally setting ourselves up for success. When the people you meet, the businesses you create, and the ways you spend your time and money improve life for yourself and others, success comes easier, because other people also want to see you succeed.

You don't have to give everything you have to charity.

But you do need to consider small ways you can contribute to the world around you in the ways you think would make the biggest positive impact.

> *List three ways you can make a positive contribution to the world around you. Choose the one you think will make the biggest impact and take the first action steps toward it right now.*

UNDERSTANDING THE POWER OF CONTRIBUTION

> *"When you cease to make a contribution, you begin to die."*
> —ELEANOR ROOSEVELT

I have seen the power of contribution and the impact it has on people's lives. It's a very important part of working to secure a positive and inspired way of living. If we keep all the good things we do focused on ourselves, over time, we feel more and more isolated.

The last thing we want to do here is isolate ourselves from the world around us.

The safest and wisest thing to do is use the power we have to benefit others. Speaking from a spiritual point of view, this is hard to ignore. There is no way we can avoid being involved with other people and society-at-large if we truly want to live a successful life. When we contribute to others, they naturally feel more inclined to help us get the things we want. Just notice the next time someone helps you out, you naturally feel like paying them back somehow.

It's a natural state of mind to help others and contribute.

If we are always thinking of how we can help other people, our hearts and minds remain open, and compassion and understanding become a secure part of who we are. **You only need to take the time to reflect on the situations you find yourself in to see opportunities to contribute everywhere.**

Next time you are walking down the street, stop and help that homeless person out with a few of the coins in your pocket, for them it could mean the difference between a meal today and not eating until tomorrow. When you next receive that bonus at work, think about how you can give some of your money (or time) to a good cause. There are so many people out there who are more unfortunate than we are, who feel alone and isolated in the world.

There is truly nothing more valuable to life itself than a person who cares deeply for those who are living that life.

> *How would it feel if you decided to contribute more in the world? List some ways you can contribute something to society. Decide to perform one simple act of contribution and notice how it makes you feel.*

TAPPING INTO THE GIVE AND RECEIVE CYCLE

> *"The law of giving is very simple: If you want joy, give joy. If love is what you seek, offer love. If you crave material wealth, help others become prosperous."*

—DEEPAK CHOPRA

One of the most fundamental aspects of our life is that what we give, we get. There are some powerful universal laws at work with this one. When we learn to live in a way that provides us with the things we need, we naturally feel more complete and abundant. From here, **the only thing we can do to keep on track is to offer to help other people in the same way.** This is why so many people, myself included, write books like this. It is one of the main avenues we unlock on our journey to give back to the world.

The same powerful education we have learned and cultivated, to improve our own life, is passed on to others to help them in the same way. As a result, we feel great about helping so many people. **This is a small example of the give and receive cycle at work.** We have received so much, naturally, we want to give more. Because we give more, we feel really good about who we are and what we are doing with our lives. This good feeling comes with a greater sense of purpose, which in turn energizes us, so we can achieve more, get more, and give even more.

It's an infinite cycle of positivity.

And who wouldn't want to be a part of that? If everyone in the world learned to think, act, and live this way, the world would be a much nicer place to live in, and you too can be a part of that.

I admit, in the beginning, it can be difficult.

There can be so many barriers to stepping into this cycle. After all, we work so hard for what we achieve, right? Why should we spend so much time giving? The answer to that question, though it can take years to fully accept, is simply...**because we are able to do so.**

There are not that many people alive in the world who have such a high degree of abundance to be able to share so much without being left wanting. People who have so little, have hardly enough to survive, and there are so many people like this in the world right now. I have met these kinds of people, and many of them **are the nicest people you could ever hope to meet**, and many of them do share the very last of what they have with others. It is truly inspiring to see a homeless person give away his possessions in the hope of helping another. And it is more than upsetting to see people walk by who obviously have more than enough to survive, and they don't even stop to consider helping in some way.

I know these people have their own life, and they make their own choices, but I have a life too, and I make the choice to help. The reward that I get from this cannot be put into words. It is a part of my spiritual journey and something I care deeply about. What I get from this is worth more than any paycheck I have ever or could ever get. It is the reward of connection; it is the reward of goodness and kindness, and knowing I made a difference in someone's life when I had the chance to. I honestly believe it's more important than keeping what I earn to myself.

What would activating the give and receive cycle mean for your life? Write out the ways you can begin

*to tap into the give and receive cycle. Then go out
and do something good for people who really need
the help.*

AUTOMATICALLY GIVING

"No one has ever become poor by giving."

—ANNE FRANK

To become completely harmonized with everything this
way of life has to offer, we can set ourselves up to automatically give back to the community-at-large. Mastery
of this art comes when we can earn ourselves a living that
naturally benefits others.

This is a very powerful truth.

A simple way of doing this is through giving away a percentage of what you earn to others. When you give to
others, the cycle of abundance doesn't end with you. **It can
flow through you, into the lives of others.** So, not only
are you receiving the benefits of a truly abundant lifestyle,
you are helping others achieve exactly the same thing.

You don't have to give away everything. You can just set
yourself up to contribute 3 percent, 5 percent, or 10 percent of your income or more. Give whatever feels right
to you.

This way, you won't be reducing your own capacity for abundance.

If you earned $500 this week, that's just $15 to $25. Even this small amount can make a difference in the life of someone who has very little. This is one of the most powerful things I have come to understand throughout my journey up to now. Automatically giving becomes just as much a part of you as your hair, or your legs, or your eyes.

If you set yourself up to give automatically, you will find that your resources increase. Not only will you feel really good about what you do, but when others find out you do this, they will want to support you even more. This can lead to an increase in income, greater opportunities to influence your reality, and even the chance to be involved with some really worthwhile causes.

What will be different in your life if you set yourself up to automatically give? Work out what percentage of your income you can easily afford to give away. Then choose what cause you want to donate your money to. This can be a single person, a group of people, a business, a charity, or literally anything you like.

CLOSING THOUGHTS

....

I hope this book has helped you take control of your life, one piece at a time in just a few minutes each day. I've shown you the tools you need to set goals, define your actions, and quickly achieve success. We've talked about how a positive mindset and consistent daily action is imperative to success.

We've covered the importance of your personal health, developing the right body mindset, cultivating more energy, and developing the mindset to consistent daily action. We've covered how purpose and passion intersect, and how to align our life with our personal purpose to lead toward peace and happiness. We've discussed how to work hard and play even harder.

We've worked through emotions (both positive and negative) and overcome fears and doubts. We've grown our positive mindset by removing negative sources, including toxic relationships. And we've learned how to develop a more inspired and positive emotional mindset that we can use to achieve our goals.

You've learned how to make more money, save more money, and how to have your money work smarter for you. We've covered how to set goals, define necessary actions, and how to bring action to success. You've learned the importance of designing a legacy that stands the test of time, by working to improve life for everyone and not just yourself.

We've looked at the importance of aligning your career or business goals with your path of personal development, and how to take action in these areas to manifest what you want. You've discovered how finding your family and friends can contribute to your personal success and the importance of connecting with them. We've discussed relationships and love, and how to cultivate positive relationship energy. We've covered defining relationships, setting deal breakers, attracting an ideal partner, and growing love and respect in intimate relationships.

We've looked at the nature of our spirituality and how to connect to Source, and how to begin to utilize our connection to Source to bring about great positive changes in our own lives and the lives of the people we meet and work with. You've learned how to contribute to something that is bigger than ourselves, how to have a lasting positive impact on the world around us, and how to cultivate a life that lets us live to the fullest possible potential. I've shown you how to compound your daily consistent action into success—your success.

Now, just keep doing it.

Keep working toward your goals with daily consistent action, and you'll soon be living your ideal life, no matter how you define it.

Now, get to it.

Just three minutes a day.

You've got this.

I love you.

Regan x

ABOUT THE
AUTHOR

....

REGAN HILLYER is a serial entrepreneur, philanthropist, mindset coach, and global speaker. She is the founder of Regan Hillyer International, a company dedicated to providing personal development and business training to those with a big message to share. Regan has trained thousands of people and helped them build six- and seven-figure businesses using powerful mindset changing tools and cutting-edge business development strategies. As a certified Master of NLP, Master of Hypnosis, Time Dynamics Specialist, and a Success Strategist, Regan has invested over $1 million in her personal development and business journey and takes pride in continuously learning from key industry leaders.

Made in the USA
Columbia, SC
08 October 2023

24125014R00126